ADVENTURES *of a* HOLLYWOOD SECRETARY

University of California Press   BERKELEY   LOS ANGELES   LONDON

ADVENTURES *of a* HOLLYWOOD SECRETARY

HER PRIVATE LETTERS FROM INSIDE THE STUDIOS OF THE 1920s

Letters of VALERIA BELLETTI

Edited and Annotated by CARI BEAUCHAMP

Frontispiece: Valeria (left) and Irma. Courtesy of Margery Baragona.

University of California Press, one of the most distinguished
university presses in the United States, enriches lives around the
world by advancing scholarship in the humanities, social sciences,
and natural sciences. Its activities are supported by the UC Press
Foundation and by philanthropic contributions from individuals
and institutions. For more information, visit
www.ucpress.edu.

University of California Press
Berkeley and Los Angeles, California

University of California Press, Ltd.
London, England

© 2006 by Cari Beauchamp

Library of Congress Cataloging-in-Publication Data

Belletti, Valeria, 1898–1959.
Adventures of a Hollywood secretary : her private letters from
inside the studios of the 1920s / letters of Valeria Belletti ; edited
and annotated by Cari Beauchamp.
    p.   cm.
Includes bibliographical references and index.
ISBN 0-520-24551-2 (cloth : alk. paper).
ISBN 0-520-24780-9 (pbk. : alk. paper)
1. Motion picture industry—California—Los Angeles—Anecdotes.
2. Belletti, Valeria, 1898–1959—Correspondence.   3. Secretaries—
United States—Correspondence.   I. Beauchamp, Cari   II. Title.
PN1993.5.U65B45   2006
384'.80979494—dc22   2005028157

Manufactured in the United States of America

15   14   13   12   11   10   09   08   07   06
    10   9   8   7   6   5   4   3   2   1

This book is printed on New Leaf EcoBook 60, containing
60% post-consumer waste, processed chlorine free; 30% de-inked
recycled fiber, elemental chlorine free; and 10% FSC-certified
virgin fiber, totally chlorine free. EcoBook 60 is acid-free and
meets the minimum requirements of ANSI/ASTM D5634–01
(*Permanence of Paper*). ♾

FOR KEVIN BROWNLOW

THE GUIDING LIGHT

FOREWORD

....

I was absolutely fascinated by Valeria's letters and am delighted that her heirs saved this extraordinary slice of history. It is most fortunate that this material found its way into the very capable hands of Cari Beauchamp.

Here is a remarkable account of the early days of the movie business told from the unique perspective of a Hollywood secretary, something we've never seen before. Her description of the day-to-day life at the studios gives a very revealing portrait of my father.

She worked in the movie business at a revolutionary time, the end of the silents and the beginning of the talkies. Despite the fact the she wrote these letters eighty years ago, her experiences often parallel those of the people working in the industry today. We're still looking for good stories, movie stars still command the public's attention, and technology is changing at a rapid clip. She perfectly captures the job description of today's Hollywood assistants when she writes, "I have to talk, talk, talk all day long. People are constantly wanting to see Mr. Goldwyn about getting into pictures or they have 'a marvelous story' that they can't mail to the office, but must see Mr. Goldwyn personally about it." Plus ça change . . .

Valeria certainly did not suffer fools gladly and knew how to live life fully. It is quite delicious to be privy to letters that were certainly not written for posterity and essentially to eavesdrop on her conversations with her dear friend Irma.

Samuel Goldwyn, Jr.

LOS ANGELES IN 1924 was still coming into its own. It had been Spanish territory a century and a half earlier when Franciscan friars cut a swath through the native villages and built the mission and plaza that soon formed the nucleus of the pueblo of Los Angeles. There was a brief Mexican reign before California was "proclaimed for America" in 1846, but while the gold rush that stimulated statehood in 1850 made a huge impact on Northern California, turning San Francisco into a major cosmopolitan city, Los Angeles remained a "tough cow town."

It wasn't until the land boom of the late 1800s that major changes grew visible, and soon midwestern families were joining together to buy hundreds of acres, moving en masse to the area to create their own communities infused with their own values. The discovery and exploitation of oil accelerated the changes, spurring the development of the port and interspersing lean-to refineries and wells among the orange groves, the churches, a few hotels, and clusters of houses and shops. By the beginning of the new century, the Southland was a series of three dozen incorporated towns, and it was close to impossible to know where one began and another ended. The region was tied together by the Red Cars, electric trains running from San Fernando down to Newport Beach and from Riverside out to the Pacific Ocean, providing cheap, easy access from one town to the next for tourists and residents alike.

The sun, the dry air, and the ocean all factored into bringing the new phenomenon of moviemaking slowly but surely to the area. Los Angeles had been introduced to "flickers" in 1896 when the lights dimmed at the Orpheum Theater, and the image of a life-sized Anna Belle Sun danced for a few precious moments on a large white sheet. It would be another decade before the filmmakers themselves arrived in earnest.

It was a young business, initially driven by immigrants, Jews, and women — talented, ambitious, and creative souls unwelcome in more respectable professions. If moviemaking was looked down upon as less than reputable, and it was, individuals on the fringes of that community were the ones who first came to Los Angeles. They were seeking refuge from the Trust, the name commonly given to the Motion Picture Patents Company controlled by Thomas Edison, which mandated license fees for the use of its patented cameras and projectors. The rising demand for movies and the corresponding increase in theaters made enforcement a challenge; renegade companies fled to Florida, Cuba, and California to dodge the Trust's vigilantes.

By 1915 the Trust was beaten, and Los Angeles was the burgeoning center of filmmaking. Movies were no longer an idea one week, in front of the cameras the next, and in theaters within a month, but the locals were none too thrilled to see women walking the streets in heavy makeup, cameras using parades as a backdrop, and men sitting under trees in biblical costumes. Yet what initially was greeted with shock and disdain gradually turned to civic pride as moviemaking became the city's largest source of jobs. The ripple effect on the hotels and restaurants and on tourism became not only appreciated but, by 1920, depended upon.

Barns and empty lots had given way to more permanent filming locations, and by 1924 large studios were a part of the landscape. Along Melrose Avenue and Gower Street, the huge United Studios abutted the much smaller FBO. The Warner brothers were up on Sunset Boulevard, and

Universal City had been flourishing in the San Fernando Valley since 1915. Metro Goldwyn Mayer had just opened its gates in Culver City the spring of 1924, and the following year Cecil B. DeMille took over the Ince Studio down the street on Washington Boulevard.

Roads that had been loose dirt and gravel only a few years before were now smoothly paved, and the hills above all this activity were graced with the huge HOLLYWOODLAND sign, recently constructed to promote yet another housing development.

Three hundred thousand people were calling Los Angeles home in 1910; when Valeria Belletti arrived in 1924, she was just one of the one hundred thousand who poured into the city in that year alone, bringing the population to almost one million. Like Valeria, they came to seek their fortune and a new life; for many, that meant the movies. The hopefuls who were arriving that year were the first to have grown up collecting photographs of the stars from fan magazines; Mary Pickford and her fellow luminaries of the previous decade had risen to fame without any path to follow. It had all changed very quickly.

Margarita Valeria Belletti was born in New Jersey on October 11, 1898, the only child of parents who had emigrated from Italy several years before. Her father, Giuseppe (who changed his name to Joseph when he came to America), was in construction and did well enough to buy a house in West New York, New Jersey, but he never adjusted well to his new home. The family visited Italy together when Valeria was two, and shortly thereafter Giuseppe went back alone and stayed there. When Valeria was ten, she and her mother, Giuseppina, visited him in Italy but returned to New Jersey after a few months.

Valeria and her mother both suffered in the cold weather, but as Valeria

3

later reflected, "even though it was within our means to make a change, we just stayed because we didn't have the courage of making a change." Yet they had enough courage to make their home without the constant presence of a husband or father and instead lived with Giuseppina's sister and her children.

When Valeria was almost sixteen, she left school and went to work in Manhattan for Lawrence and Herbert Langner, who were opening their own international patent practice. Lawrence Langner was soon dividing his time between his professional work and his first love, the theater, and, as the founder of the Theater Guild, he would become a prime mover behind Broadway in the twenties, thirties, and forties.

In 1914 Valeria was the Langner brothers' one and only secretary, but during the ten years she worked for them, their business grew to include half a dozen partners and offices in Chicago, Washington, London, Paris, and Berlin. Langner described Valeria as "unusually bright" in his autobiography, *The Magic Lantern*, and although she rose to be put in charge of their annuity department, she was still little more than a glorified stenographer. For women the glass ceiling was still in the future; there was a steel ceiling that limited them to little beyond a secretarial role.

Yet Valeria enjoyed her work; she "hero worshipped" her boss, who was polite and considerate and communicative, all qualities she would find lacking in her later employers, especially Sam Goldwyn. At the Langners', she was grateful for the opportunity to work in the city and to take advantage of all that New York had to offer, including free theater tickets provided by her boss. It was the era of the royal "we"; she felt she was an integral part of their business even though the Langners were making a fortune and she was taking home $25 a week.

For a while her life in New York was enough for her, with her interesting job, social events, and friends to share it all with. Valeria proudly marched in suffragette parades supporting the vote for women before the Nineteenth Amendment became law in 1920. With her short brown hair and her blue eyes, she was always on the lookout for a good time — within the bounds of propriety of course — and for a man to enjoy it with. She was very much a young woman of her times, proper but curious, taking her work seriously and ambitious to a point, but always wondering if the next man she met was husband material.

By the early 1920s the Great War had been over for several years and the Jazz Age was in full swing. Valeria was the first to say she was "conventional" and "prim," even "a little too narrow," but she was glad of it because she also saw herself as adventurous, certainly in relation to some of her friends, who were content to live their lives without going to see the newest stage show or latest club or traveling outside their own little worlds. As Valeria entered her midtwenties without finding a man she was seriously interested in, she shared confidences with several close girlfriends. One of the best was Irma Prina, who also worked in Manhattan, at the office of her family's produce business. The girls had known each other since childhood.

In early 1923 Valeria's mother died, at the age of fifty-one. Valeria stayed on with her aunt and cousins in New Jersey, but she began to reevaluate her situation. She and Irma had been talking for some time about taking a trip to California; Irma had relatives in Berkeley, near San Francisco, and if not now, when? As they began planning in earnest, Valeria realized she had little to hold her in New York; her mother was dead, her father was in Italy. Everyone said the West was good for your health, and she had long suffered from asthma. Valeria decided she would stay on in California if she liked it.

She shared her thinking with Lawrence Langner, who said he hated to see her go but wrote her a glowing letter of recommendation and several letters of introduction to friends in California. He assured her that if she changed her mind, he would welcome her back, but the more Valeria thought about it, the more sure she was that she was ready for a new adventure. After all, at twenty-five she wasn't getting any younger and if she was ever going to make a change, now was the time.

Valeria and Irma took the train west and shared a fabulous summer, visiting San Francisco and the Bay Area and then traveling on to Santa Barbara, Los Angeles, and San Diego. They looked like Mutt and Jeff, with Irma at five feet nine inches and tiny Valeria, who didn't hit five feet. But together they were downright daring for two women traveling alone — they took a boat to Catalina and flew in a plane over Coronado in San Diego. In September they returned north to Berkeley, where they stayed with Irma's aunt and where Mr. Langner had contacts. Valeria considered staying there, but she had been enchanted by the weather and the palm trees of Los Angeles. She and Irma parted company in Berkeley, with Irma packing to return to the East Coast as Valeria headed south again. She checked into the Los Angeles YWCA and, armed with a hundred dollars and her letters from Langner, set out to make a new life.

Our story begins with Valeria's first letter to Irma that fall.

....

OCT. 12, 1924
SUNDAY MORNING
Dear Irma,

Well, I'm back in Los Angeles and am rooming for the time being with 2 other girls in the Y.W.[C.A.] as they had no private rooms. These girls seem to be very nice and in a way it's better that I'm not alone. Although I feel much better, my cold is loosened up and of course I have to cough quite a bit, and you know how you feel in public when your cold is in that stage. These girls in my room are awfully considerate and have offered everything they have to help me get over it.

I slept until 11:30 this morning and the girls have just gone out for breakfast. They told me not to bother to get dressed but just stay in bed and they are bringing me toast and coffee. You see Irma, one is not always out of luck, you usually find people who are willing to lend you a hand.

It's quite warm here today so that in the afternoon I'll sit in the sun on the porch and then go to bed early.

On the train from Barstow I met a fellow who was awfully nice to me, even though he saw that I was not so well and quite unsociable. He carried my suitcase for me and he saw me to the Y.W. He wanted to take me out today but I told him I couldn't because I wanted to doctor myself and get well as soon as possible. This fellow's name is Jack Purcell and is a chef for the Fred Harvey people. He said that if I wanted to he would speak to one of the head men to get me a position so that I could travel from place to place and in that way see all the resorts. This fellow seems awfully good hearted, but as usual I don't like him very much so that I hope he doesn't call me up.

How is everything in West Berkeley? I'd like to hear from you and if you'll write me care of the YWCA at 200 S. Vermont Street I'll get your mail because I think I'll stay here for at least a week.

With kind regards to your aunt and uncle, I am

Yours,
Valeria

Dear Irma,

Tonight is so beautiful. The moon is so big and yellow and looks like a picture through the trees in front of my window. I'm beginning to get romantic again in this warm climate.

The two girls in my room are out—one with a boy friend and the other has to work nights as she is telegraph operator.

I didn't mind staying here by myself today because there is an auditorium right next to my window and the opera singers here in Los Angeles are practicing for 2 weeks. They tell me that they practice here every day during their stay so that I expect to be entertained for nothing for the rest of the week.

If I see Catherine I'll tell her about your leaving the 20th and of course I'll write you as soon as I see her. With kind regard to all, I am,

Yours,
Valeria

OCTOBER 31, 1924

Dear Irma,

I suppose your trip to California is now a thing of the past and you are down to business again. How does West New York look after beautiful California?

I'm still here at the Y and feel splendid. I've gotten a job working only half day, that is, from 1 to 5 in the afternoon and off all day Saturday. I'm assistant to a big doctor (one of those nature and drugless doctors) here in Los Angeles. He writes articles called "Care of the Body" in the Los Angeles Times and he's also writing books.

He's quite clever and has an immune practice. My job is a cinch; all I have to do is write a few letters in reply to letters from people asking what to do in regard to their ailments; write out the dietary lists for the patients; escort them into their treating rooms; collect fees and make appointments.

The doctor has left the management of the business end of the office entirely in my hands because he says he knows nothing about business. He told me that what was the most important thing was that I should be pleasant to all the patients who come in and talk to them. I have to wear a nurse's outfit and he's also given me a book on Hydro-Therapy that he wants me to study.

I'm getting $50 a month for just sitting around being pleasant, etc. and if I'm the girl he wants, I'll work all day. By the 1st of the year he'll give me $150 and after I've learned enough about diets, etc. that I can answer the mail myself, he said he'd give me $300. Of course, you can't believe all they tell you, but I'll stick to it for the time being because I have all morning to myself and the weekends and I make enough to pay my room and board. I'm also learning a lot about what to eat and how to live.

I'm writing this letter while I'm eating my breakfast, squatted on the bed. My breakfast consists of 3 bran muffins, a half pound of grapes and one apple and 4 glasses of water. The doctor says if I follow his instructions, I'll be real strong in about 3 months. I also have to do some exercises and walk as much as possible. It almost seems like fate or whatever it is that I should get into a place like that when I really came out to California to learn how to live and get real strong.

Today is simply gorgeous, the sun has been out since six this morning and everything looks so fresh and green because we had rain during the night. The Y is situated about 3 blocks from Hollywood and is partially surrounded by hills. It's quite pretty and it's out of the heart of the city. Do you remember where the University of California Southern Branch was located? Well, the Y is on the same street only a few blocks down.

How is your niece Patricia? You were so anxious to hear about her when you were here, remember? Please write to me soon and let me know how everything is.

I haven't forgotten to send you some orange blossoms, but I have yet to find out when they bloom. Please remember me to all your folks and hoping to hear from you soon, I remain,

Your Western Chum, Valeria

DECEMBER 1, 1924

Dear Irma,

Your awfully nice letter received and hungrily devoured for all the news of home you gave me. You don't say anything about your trip back East, but I presume you met with no misadventure.

Well, my job is no more. I was fired this morning. I don't know just why. It's simply a mystery and I haven't bothered to ask for an explanation. Dr. Losell's secretary called me up this morning and just said "Oh, you need not come in any more, we've decided that I can manage the office alone, without additional help. Do you want to come down for your check or shall we mail it?"

I flippantly replied "Oh, all right, mail it. I don't feel like coming downtown for it." And that ended it. I have my suspicions as to why I was fired and that's due to Dr. Losell's secretary. I noticed lately that it quite annoyed her when the doctor preferred to give me dictation and showed some interest in me. I suppose she was afraid I might eventually succeed her so she found some way of getting me ousted. I know that I did my work well, because all the articles the doctor dictates to me I got out without a mistake and further more, so far as I could see, he was quite pleased with the way I handled matters and let me have full sway of the business end of the office. That's one more experience added to my life—that of being fired. I often had wondered how it felt—now I know.

I believe I have another job, but won't say definitely until I'm working. I'm to start a week from today, and it's only a temporary position for 3 months. One of the men whom I was introduced to, Mr. Joseph P. Loeb, by Lawrence Langner, called me up last week and wanted to know if I could be his secretary for 3 months as his secretary is leaving on a 3 month vacation. I told him at the time that I couldn't as I already had a job. This morning when I was notified that I was fired, I called up Mr. Loeb and asked him if the position was still open. He said it was and that I should see him tomorrow for an interview and then start work next Monday. Mr. Loeb is a member of the firm of Loeb, Walker and Loeb, corporation lawyers who represent all the big movie companies. They have wonderful offices and so far as I can see I believe the change will be for the better, even if temporary.

I certainly did learn an awful lot at Dr. Losell's office. He took such pains with me to see that I learned all about the body and whenever he could he would tell me the cause of various illnesses and their cure. He also gave me information concerning matters which I had been entirely ignorant of, and in fact taught me how to live right. In a way, I'm sorry that I had to leave him, but on the other hand, I also had some disagreeable tasks. He was just breaking me in to assist him in examinations and while some were alright, there were some examinations that I didn't quite like to witness. He told me beforehand that I'd have to forget all my prudery in doing this work, but you know Irma, it's hard to do it when you've been brought up the way we girls have.

I suppose you all had a wonderful time Thanksgiving. I did too. A woman I met some time ago in a restaurant invited me to her home for Thanksgiving and I must say that I enjoyed myself.

I don't know if I already told you, but Eva (a girl I met in the Y and whom I have now made a friend and chum of) and I have a lovely apartment in Hollywood. It's much nicer than the one in the Buckingham Apartments because everything is clean and new. We had quite a lot of company yesterday and had a wonderful time preparing dinner. Eva's mother came down from the ranch to spend the week end in the City and Eva's sister and husband were here too and one of Eva's beaux. Tomorrow night two friends of Eva's are coming to the home and we're going to make candy and play cards. Next weekend I believe I'm going to get a real thrill. We've made up a party of six and we're going to hike to the Sierra Madre Mountains. We're going to leave early Saturday afternoon and stay overnight at one of the mountain lodges. I'll write and tell you all about it.

I'm sorry you're not here to see the Calla lilies. They're in full bloom and so are the poinsettias. The nights here are now cooler, but the days are just the same as in September when you were here. If you ever saw my apartment and the wonderful weather, I bet you'd hate to go back to New York now. I just adore it. I look around and hardly believe it can be me in this beautiful place. We pay $50 a month for it which includes gas, electricity and private phone. We have real silverware and all aluminum pots and pans. Our sitting room is gray and old rose. Gray rug, old rose draperies (silk) floor lamp, mahogany furniture and a refectory table and big settee. All I need is a few fancy pillows and I'll get those later.

Eva's brother has a vegetable market and we get all our vegetables wholesale. Not only that, but when I go there and shop, his partner, Fred, who has a Cleveland sedan, takes me home so I don't have to carry the parcels. Eva's mother and sister have brought us about 5 jars of preserved fruit and 3 jars of jelly. We also have walnuts left from the other weekend when we went to the ranch and picked about 10 pounds. Since we're vegetarians you see that it costs us very little so far to live.

We have quite an illustrious neighbor, Ben Turpin.* I saw him sitting on the porch this morning with his son, but I wouldn't have known it was him had I not known that he lived in that house. We live near the big Fox studios and you run into some funny characters on the street. They come off the lot in their make up and outfits so that you see cowboys, old gents with long hair, looking like the 49'ers; men in society clothes and in fact all kinds of rig-outs. This sure is a queer burg, but I like it better than Los Angeles. It's nearer the mountains and is higher so that the air seems better than in L.A. It takes me about 40 minutes to get into Los Angeles and the fare is only 5 cents.

I passed in front of Grauman's Egyptian Theater† this morning and it's being fixed over for the opening of "Romola" on December

---

*Ben Turpin was a popular vaudeville and silent screen comedian who worked with Charlie Chaplin and Mack Sennett. Turpin was known for his slapstick and ludicrous impressions, enhanced by the fact that he was cross-eyed.

†The success of theatrical impresario Sid Grauman's Egyptian Theater led him to open his Chinese Theater down the block on Hollywood Boulevard in 1927.

6. It's going to be a gala affair and wish that I could go, but I guess I have a small chance of getting in on opening night.

Have you been to any shows lately? Tell me about them if you have. Give my love to all and write soon.

Valeria

JANUARY 20, 1925

Dear Irma,

I received your letter and want to thank you especially for the clipping showing the new Theater Guild building which of course interested me exceedingly.

Well, Irma, I'm sure having the time of my life. I feel as if I were truly living. The weather just now is glorious. It's neither too warm nor too cold and the sun is so bright that I just want to be out all the time.

I'm working for Mr. Loeb as his secretary. We are the legal advisors of all the big movie concerns for the stars so of course I'm getting to know all the ins and outs of the movie industry as well as the scandals, etc.

I get $27.50 a week and that goes a long way here. The apartment I had with Eva is no more as Eva left me for a man. However, I've found 2 other girls—one works in my office and the other is an art teacher. The 3 of us have one of those Spanish type bungalows—we pay $65 a month and it's furnished beautifully. We have a back and front door entrance and French windows in our sitting room. I'm going to learn how to ride a horse because both girls go riding every Sunday.

There's a beautiful natural park (about 4,000 acres) in the Hollywood hills where the girls go. The riding club they belong to is very
reasonable ($10 a month entitles you to a 2 hour lesson every Sun-
day). The girls also play golf so that I've got to learn that too. We
also go swimming one night a week so you see I'm becoming an all
around athlete.

Now for some real news. Whom do you suppose I met in Hollywood 3 weeks ago? None other than Miss Franklin. We have become
very chummy and I've spent many evenings at her apartment. She's
an entirely different girl than she was when we first met her. In
fact she's almost like a fairy god mother to me. She says she likes
me an awful lot and proceeds to shower me with all sorts of attentions—takes me to dinner and shows and absolutely insists on paying
for everything. She isn't working and hasn't a profession, but she
must have quite a large income because I wish you'd see the clothes
she has bought since she's been in Los Angeles. Not only that, but
she pays $65 for an apartment for herself. I spent New Years with her
and stayed over night at their apartment and went on an all day trip
to Santa Ana. The truth is I seem to spend more time in her apartment than in my own. Miss Franklin used to be an actress; played in
a number of musical comedies on the Orpheum circuit and finally in
stock in Denver. However, due to a fall from a horse six years ago,
she was confined for almost a year; that caused her to get fat and so
ended her career.

I have run out of paper so am forced to conclude my letter
abruptly. I hope you are all well and happy and that you won't forget
to write to me soon.

Love, Valeria

FEB 19, 1925

Dear Irma,

I just had to write to you to tell you of my good fortune. I'm in the movies—of course, not an actress. I'm private and social secretary to Mr. Samuel Goldwyn. Can you imagine it! The odds were about 50 to 1 against me, but through Mr. Loeb's influence, the position was given to me. So far as I can see, it's the sort of job that I've always dreamed about, but that I never, by any stretch of imagination, hoped to get.

As Mr. Goldwyn's secretary, I come in contact with every phase of the movie industry; looking for new material; keeping in touch with the producers in New York; reading new books; turning over possible material to the scenario writer who happens to be Frances Marion; hiring actors and actresses, directors, camera men; keeping in touch with the art director, publicity man, the projection and cutting rooms and ever so many other things. Everything is so new and interesting that I just love to work. Of course, I am not busy just now, because Mr. Goldwyn is in Europe and we've just finished a picture called "His Supreme Moment" with Ronald Colman and we don't start another production until the first of May, which will be "Stella Dallas." We're only starting to look for a cast suitable for the characters of the play and things won't be ready for actual shooting until May. I'm working in Hollywood of course, and it's too bad you can't come out to the coast now, because I could get you in the studios to see everything.

I met Mr. George Fitzmaurice today. He does all our society pictures. I also met Ronald Colman who is a very charming young man. Have you seen him in pictures yet? His latest was "A Thief in Paradise."

I wish you could see the studios inside. They are a town in themselves. We have named streets and different shops, such as barber shops, beauty parlors and cafes. Yesterday I didn't have much to do, so I walked around the lot and watched different pictures being taken. Did you know that a regular three piece string orchestra is on each set in order to produce the necessary emotions in the stars? I enjoyed listening to the music more than watching the acting.

Mr. Lehr, who is the general manager, told me that as Mr. Goldwyn's secretary I would have to look very smart and dress well. He told me that if I needed any money for this purpose he would be glad to give it to me and pay him back when I could. Mr. Loeb told me the same thing. Really, it is astounding how free people are with their money here. He gave me the afternoon off to do whatever shopping I needed to do and I certainly did go to it. I bought so much that I feel as if I'm a different person entirely. For once in my life I bought real stylish clothes and they do make a difference. Of course, I have to keep my hair marcelled, but in view of the salary I am being paid, I can easily do it.

My salary to start with is $40.00 a week and when we go in production on May 1st, my salary will be $50 because I'll be much busier. The girl who had my job was getting $65 and she had been with Mr. Goldwyn only 9 months. She left because she was ordered to go away for a long rest cure due to a lung infection.

I'm just reading a book called "Ann's an Idiot." It's not one of the very latest, but it is fairly modern. That's part of my job, but as I've been reading for about an hour, I thought I'd quit a while to write you this letter because on account of it being a rainy day, there's little going on and the general manager has left for the day.

I don't know how long my job will last—it all depends on whether or not Mr. Goldwyn likes me. I'm told that he is very temperamental and rather difficult to get along with. However, I'm rather accustomed to temperamental people so that will be nothing new to me. Even if I do get fired when he gets back, I will have enjoyed my short stay and will have gotten a slight knowledge of the movie industry.

I have become very friendly with a Miss Manee who is Mr. Maurice Tourneur's secretary and reader. She is very intellectual and has read so much that I feel positively stupid in her presence. However, she seems to like me because she keeps inviting me to lunch with her.

By the way, I wish you'd see the little cafe we eat in. It is so picturesque. You see people (mostly men) in all kinds of make up and costumes and of course there are no outsiders at all. Just movie folks. It is surprising how few girls there are on a studio lot. I just can't seem to get used to all the men. None of them are very interesting; and most of them are just types that I couldn't possibly make an effort to be friendly with. I did meet one chap who seemed awfully nice—he was Dr. Gardner's chauffeur. As I was leaving the studio yesterday afternoon, a car came out of the gate and stopped and this fellow asked me if I was going to Los Angeles; I said I was so he invited me to ride with him, which of course I accepted. The car he was driving was a new Rolls Royce and believe me I felt big driving through Los Angeles in it. I hope I meet him again.

I'm still living with Florence and Nancy in our Bungalow. We have rented a piano and we have some real nice times at home.

Florence brings over some of the men teachers in her school and Nancy has some of her boyfriends come over. When they come they always bring some good stuff to drink and we make cocktails and dance or play bridge. The boys are really nice fellows, that is, good morally, so that you need not worry that I have left the straight and narrow. We all go out together and we've been to a number of real wild bohemian cafes in Hollywood. It's fun watching and I'm also gaining quite some experience in the way of mankind.

I'm feeling perfectly splendid and am all enthused and pepped up. You have no idea how glad I am I left New York. Now I realize what a rut I was in when I was home. Here I've been meeting all kinds of interesting people and although I miss Mr. Langner and all my friends in Jersey, I feel that I'm enjoying life more here. Another thing, I don't know whether it is the sunshine or just what it is, but I feel much more carefree and lighthearted. After all, I believe it is one's duty to seek and if possible find happiness and that is my aim.

Give my regards to your folks and let me hear from you real soon.

Love, Valeria

....

Sam Goldwyn was unique among Hollywood studio moguls in the 1920s. Louis B. Mayer ran MGM with his production chief, Irving Thalberg, and turned out forty films a year; Adolph Zukor and Jesse Lasky made a similar number of films at Paramount. They, along with the likes of William Fox at his own studio and Carl Laemmle at Universal, were creating moviemaking factories. Goldwyn alone was at the other end of the continuum, producing films one at a time and using the profits from the last film to pay for the next one. As his biographer, A. Scott Berg, describes Goldwyn's reality, "He was eating caviar but living hand to mouth."

Sam Goldwyn had been born Schmuel Gelbfisz in Warsaw in 1879 and began his immigration westward by walking to Hamburg. From there, it was to London (where he became Samuel Goldfish) and then to America at the age of twenty. He found work as a glove maker in upstate New York, where he and Abe Lehr, the son of the factory owner, were benchmates. (By 1924, Abe Lehr would be Sam's studio manager, not for his film expertise, but because Sam trusted him completely.)

Sam rapidly rose from glove maker to salesman, even returning to visit Europe in his capacity as one of the company's leading salesmen. He was in the process of moving to Manhattan when he met and married Blanche Lasky there in 1910. Blanche and her brother, Jesse, had been vaudevillians, and soon Sam and Jesse joined together to form the Jesse L. Lasky Feature Play Company and began making movies. Their first, *The Squaw Man,* was directed by the inexperienced but enthusiastic Cecil B. DeMille in 1913 and was the first feature film shot entirely in Los Angeles. When they ran out of money before it was finished, Sam stepped in and showed the bluff and bluster that would make him a great in the industry: he "presold" *The Squaw Man* as the first of twelve films from their company to various distributors and exhibitors and, in the process, raised enough money to finish the movie. It was also Sam who saved the day when the first reels were screened and the film jumped all over the place. Goldwyn found the film laboratory that could solve the problem by fixing the sprocket holes on the cheap stock they had purchased, which were not correctly punched for the standard projector.

Sam and Jesse joined forces with Adolph Zukor to create Famous Players—Lasky in 1916 but Sam, already resentful of Lasky and DeMille's getting most of the publicity, soon resented Zukor as well. Even though Sam was chairman of the new company, he didn't get along with Zukor or his leading lady, Mary Pickford, and they responded in kind. When Sam went to his brother-in-law and said, "It's Zukor or me," Jesse chose Zukor. Sam never forgave him and left the whole Lasky family behind; Blanche divorced him in 1916 on the grounds of adultery, three years after the birth of their daughter, Ruth, whom Sam ignored for the next two decades.

Sam's next move was to partner with the Selwyn brothers and, combining portions of their surnames, they formed Goldwyn Productions (as it was pointed out at the time, the other alternative was "Selfish Productions"). Soon after, *Photoplay* ran a black-bordered picture of Sam Goldfish, explaining "Not dead, but legally annihilated," as a New York court had granted his request to use the company name as his own new last name. The Goldwyn Company expanded to buy the Triangle Studios in Culver City, but the investors insisted on new management and, once again, Sam was out. He had burned so many bridges that there was simply no one left to partner with. As Irene Selznick, daughter of Louis B. Mayer and wife of producer David O. Selznick, said about Sam: "Even those fondest of him agreed he was impossible."

If Goldwyn wanted to keep making films, he had to go it alone. His old friend Cecil B. DeMille and his new friend Joe Schenck helped Sam get financing from the Bank of Italy, where both men were on the board of advisors. Next, Goldwyn needed a director, and he signed a profit-sharing agreement with Paris-born George Fitzmaurice, still in his late twenties but already an experienced director. After graduating from art school, Fitzmaurice entered the film business through Pathé, writing such serials as *The Perils of Pauline*. He had organized the London studios for Famous Players–Lasky before coming to work for Sam, where he directed the new company's first film, the ethnic comedy *Potash and Perlmutter*, in 1923.

Goldwyn made a deal to distribute his films through First National, a consortium of various theater circuits that also produced its own films at the United Studios on Melrose Avenue. Goldwyn's company made its films there as well until the studio was sold to Paramount in 1926 (Paramount still operates out of the same studio today).

Goldwyn added Henry King, thirty-seven, as his second contracted director just before Valeria came to the studio. Born and raised in Virginia, King had joined a touring stock company as a teenager and traveled the country as an actor in a variety of productions. Like so many others, he entered filmmaking through a fluke encounter; escorting a friend to a meeting at Lubin Studios in New York in 1912, he was recruited on the spot to appear before the camera. King appeared in dozens of films, but by 1917 he had switched over to directing. After two years with Thomas Ince, King formed his own production company and hit gold with *Tol'able David* in 1921; such acclaimed films as *Sonny* and *The White Sister* followed.

According to King, Goldwyn had first approached him about working together back in 1919, but Goldwyn's patronizing attitude so appalled King that he announced, "I wouldn't work for this man under any circumstances." Yet six years later, King and Goldwyn both employed the attorney Nathan Burkan, and the three men met together at the Ambassador Hotel to see if they could come to an agreement. Burkan turned to King and said, "Henry, this man will carry out to the letter every word there is in a contract he signs, but don't believe anything he tells you or promises you that isn't written." Goldwyn protested, but Burkan calmly said he was simply telling the truth. King was convinced, made sure the contract spelled out everything he cared about, and signed a combination salary and percentage deal.

King brought with him one of the few actors Goldwyn put under contract, Ronald Colman. The English-born Colman had attended Cambridge, served in World War I, and acted in school and on the British stage before heading to America in 1922 at the age of twenty-eight. He was acting on Broadway when he was seen by Henry King, who cast Colman in his first American film, *The White Sister*, opposite Lillian Gish. Shortly thereafter, both King and Colman joined Goldwyn.

Sam's only contracted writer was Frances Marion, who had been Hollywood's highest-paid screenwriter since 1915. She had risen to fame and fortune as Mary Pickford's exclusive screenwriter, turning out such hits as *Poor Little Rich Girl*, *Rebecca of Sunnybrook Farm*, and *The Little Princess*. Since 1919, Frances had preferred the freedom of working from assignment to assignment and, in the process, had written scripts for the likes of Marion Davies, Norma and Constance Talmadge, Douglas Fairbanks, and Colleen Moore. Frances Marion had more than one hundred filmed scripts to her credit by 1923 and could handle just about anyone, but friends cautioned her about Sam Goldwyn. They said he was a ridiculous taskmaster with no taste, and she had better study voice projection in preparation for what they warned would be daily shouting matches.

Intrigued by a good challenge and lured by Sam's willingness to pay her asking price of $2,000 a week and his agreement that she wouldn't be exclusively tied to him, Frances said she went to work with her "mental boxing gloves" at the ready. Instead, she found that while he was exhausting to work with, both physically and mentally, her respect for Goldwyn grew over time. "There was never any pretense about him. He always worked harder than anyone he ever hired and his appreciation for a job well done [was] always immense and completely genuine."

Still, Frances Marion had a seasoned career behind her, other choices ahead of her, and a multitude of friends to support her. For Valeria, it was the only job she had. While a few people had dropped hints about what Goldwyn was like to work for, she had to discover it herself on a day-by-day basis. The one thing Valeria had going for her at the moment was that

Goldwyn was gone from the studio for another few months and she could learn all about the place and get to know all the other players before actually meeting her new boss.

FEBRUARY 27, 1925

1520 3/5 REID ST., LOS ANGELES, CALIF.

Dear Irma,

I just received your letter and as I have nothing to do this afternoon but read a book ("Women and Wives" by Ferguson) I thought I'd drop you a letter before I go on with the next chapter. The book is rather dull so far, but it may turn out interesting before I get through with it. I just finished "Ann's an Idiot." This book started very well, but ended like usual novels. Impossible situations and types not true to life. Ann is a very charming character and about the only reason for which the book was evidently written. (Do I sound like a real critic? I don't like to use the usual phraseology that critics use because I'd like to be original if I can. However, it's hard after having read all the criticisms I have.)

Yesterday and today have been gorgeous and as I'm sitting here typing, there's a little cricket chirping away as fast as he can. I wonder if he's trying to keep up with the clattering of my typewriter. I've just climbed out of my window to see if I can find him, but can't.

Nancy, Florence and I spent the weekend at Mount Lowe. It's too bad you didn't take that trip because it really is beautiful and I think you missed something. Perhaps the next time you come (which I hope will be real soon) we can take it together. We went on horses to the top of the mountain, and I was terribly frightened. The trail is only about 3 feet wide, perhaps less, and is on the very edge of the mountain. I had to keep my eyes closed for a time because I just couldn't look. I was dizzy from the altitude and wished for nothing more than to be on level ground. After riding about 2 hours, this sensation left me and I became more brave, and then began to enjoy the scenery. We had regular western saddles on our horses and I had a funny khaki skirt, split in the middle, so that I felt like a cowgirl. We slept in a log cabin which was cold as could be. We had a funny little stove (an antique I think) and kept putting wood in it during the night. We had to get our water outside and as you can imagine, we had no other conveniences. In spite of everything, we enjoyed it.

Listen here, where do you get that stuff about being old? Do you know what you need? You need to come to live in California. It will make you feel young. Since I've been here, I've lost ten years. I feel so wonderful, carefree and perhaps a little romantic. Your friend is right about the climate. Of course I'm not sure whether it's the sunshine or the beautiful moonlight nights, but it does have an effect.

I've seen a lot of Miss Franklin and we still are friendly although we parted for about a week. She came back however. It was like this. The three of us girls gave a little dinner party one evening to our three best fellows (ones we wanted to impress). Of course the boys brought some booze and after dinner, we prepared the cocktails. Just as we were doing this, who drops in on us without warning, but Miss Franklin. We offered her a drink, and she positively refused, and as much as said that we were not ladies because we drank a cocktail. Then to make matters worse, we started to smoke. That finished it. She was horribly surprised and asked to be taken home—which we did with pleasure. I didn't hear from her for about a week and concluded that she didn't want to have anything more to do with me. However, she evidently changed her mind and we are again friendly. She told me she was rather old fashioned in her ideas on account of having associated with older people, but after thinking it over, she saw that we were all right so now everything is O.K. and she thinks I'm still a lady, even though once in a while I have a cocktail and sometimes I smoke.

That's awfully kind of you to offer to send me papers. I haven't been getting the New York papers until I got my present job. Now I get the Sunday Telegram which I have to scan very carefully for theatrical news. The only paper I really cared for was the Morning World in order to read Heywood Broun's column and F.P.A.'s column. Of course, I know that you don't get this paper, so I wouldn't want you to get it expressly for me. However, if you see anything of interest in the papers you read, I shall appreciate your sending me clippings.

Well, I've been hob-nobbing with stars for the last week and if it doesn't bore you to hear about them, I'll be glad to tell you who I saw. I've met Blanche Sweet. She was in the office a few days ago and our general manager gave her a call down for spending too much money on clothes in the last picture she was in. I don't like her much. She's rather flippant and doesn't seem to have any personality whatsoever. Was introduced to Conway Tearle, who seems to be quite a nice chap, but wasn't with him long enough to find out anything further about him. Ran into Thomas Meighan on the lot, who is really good looking. Beautiful blue-black wavy hair, sunburned, twinkling eyes, etc. Saw Conrad Nagel in the tea room. He was seated at the next table and seems to be quite a personality, although not so good looking. Has beautiful table manners. That's all I can say about him.

Saw Claire Windsor in the tea room also.* Very good looking, but is a bleached blonde. Saw Lewis Stone today. He's adorable with his makeup on. I don't know how he looks without it. No doubt like any ordinary middle aged man. As for Ronald Colman—well—he's what I call a sheik. By the way, you know I'm his secretary too. I have to look at all his fan letters and when there are any particularly funny, I show them to him. Try to see him if you can in "A Thief in Paradise." His next picture will be "His Supreme Moment" and that will come out in the latter part of April. Mr. Colman is in New York just now. No one is supposed to know this, because he is there for a rest and doesn't want to be annoyed, however I don't see any harm in telling you. He's an Englishman, and his wife is suing him for divorce on the grounds of desertion.

Miss Frances Marion was in today. She is our scenario and continuity writer. Mr. George Fitzmaurice has his office next to mine and I see quite a lot of him. He's just finished directing *His Supreme Moment* and is going to Europe in about two weeks for a rest.

Yesterday I had to type all the titles to this picture and enjoyed doing it because it was fun. Such awful titles "If I really loved him, I'd make any sacrifice for him"; "Carla, it's you I love, dear"; "Your indifference is killing me, just love me a little." Such rot. Mr. Fitzmaurice and I laughed so at them. Today they all have gone to the projection room to see the picture fully assembled and titled and

*Because Goldwyn worked out of the huge United Studios lot, Valeria ran into stars working there for other companies.

they've all just come back ranting. The titles are impossible so they have to hire someone to write new ones.

Mr. Fitzmaurice is keen on Florence Vidor and they go out quite a lot to parties together. (Miss Vidor is divorced from her husband King Vidor).

As for my boss, Mr. Samuel Goldwyn, I've heard so much about him that there is little I can say that is nice. I'm told he's a terrible chaser. You can imagine how bad he is when his divorce decree forbids him to marry again, although the privilege was given to his ex-wife. (I have charge of all Mr. Goldwyn's personal papers, so I know whereof I speak).* I suppose as his secretary, I should not say anything more about his personal affairs, so I'll tell you about all the other scandals but his.

The gossip in Hollywood just now centers around Charlie Chaplin. You know of course about his marrying that 16 year old child.† Well, he was compelled to. You see he wronged her and she threatened to advise the police and since she was under age, why it was either marry her or go to jail. So he married her in order to save his reputation and career. When he came back to Hollywood, he brought his wife to his home and he has never gone into it since. She is there alone with the servants and is expecting a child very soon.

---

*Valeria was obviously unaware of a fairly standard clause in divorces at the time in New York, making it unlawful for the spouse accused of adultery to remarry in that state. Valeria's remarks in this instance seem to reveal more about her own curiosity and willingness to go through her boss's papers than about Sam's character.

†Chaplin had married his *Gold Rush* "find," the pregnant Lita Grey, in Mexico on November 26, 1924. He was so enthusiastic that he reportedly put Lita and her mother in the bridal suite and he stayed elsewhere. Though all of Hollywood appears to have known the facts, the baby's birth on May 5, 1925, was kept quiet and his birthday announced as June 28, the date of *The Gold Rush* premiere, to publicly hedge the necessity of the marriage.

He's been going around with Marion Davies and I think Mr. Hearst will soon cause some trouble. At least so it is rumored.

I guess that's about all I know just now, but will let you know if I hear anything more of interest.

I'm having a suit made of dark blue twill—very tailor made. Short coat, double breasted with four buttons—two in a row. I thought this would look nice for office wear. You see our offices are on the shady side, and inside it is a bit too cool to wear thin dresses. I'm also having another tailored dress made of some light colored material. I think it's tan. That's one draw back about this job. I have to look nice, and that's so hard for me because I hate to shop and worry about clothes. I told the general manager about this and he said that it would be to my advantage to look as best I could because in this work clothes mean so much. I also explained to him that I didn't like the idea of spending my whole salary on clothes and he said that perhaps for a few months I would, but after that my salary would be increased and then I could dress well and also have enough left over to save. I've never been so extravagant in my life and do you know it just seems sinful to me to spend so much on myself. I just can't do it happily.

I just must stop, because if I keep going, I'll begin to bore you (Ain't I a terrible typist—I make so many mistakes—it must be that d—— cricket. He's still chirping away and evidently his family has joined him because I hear about 4 or 5 different kinds of chirps.)

Oh, I just must tell you one more thing. Our art director, Mr. Grot, is awfully nice. He has his studio right above my room and I visit him occasionally and watch him sketch. Sometimes he won't let me in because he's sketching something he doesn't want me to see. I suppose he's afraid I'll be shocked. It's amusing to find anyone like that around a movie studio, but I rather like him. Evidently I must convey the impression to him of being a very unsophisticated, innocent young girl. Well, I'll let him think that.

How is your sister Mary? Is she feeling better? Do you think she will ever come out here? I'm glad to hear that Ida's baby is getting along so well and I presume Ida too.

Do you know, Irma, I'm so glad I came to California. Life seems more interesting to me since I've been here. I haven't been lonesome once since I've been out here and, strange to say, I have no desire to come back east.

Love, Valeria

Remember me to your mother and Isabel and the other members of your family.

MARCH 1925

Dear Irma,

I received the two packages of newspapers from you, for which I thank you a thousand times. It gave me no end of pleasure to read dear old Broun and F.P.A. again. You are indeed thoughtful, and some day you'll be rewarded.

I've just finished reading "The Keys to This City," and while I agree with Broun that it would make a good movie, we have rejected it because the lead is not quite suitable to our star, Ronald Colman. No doubt some other company will buy it—personally I think it would be a splendid part for Richard Dix—don't you?

I like my work very much, but not the people for whom I work. It's almost intolerable working for Mr. Lehr, (Mr. Goldwyn's general manager) and no doubt it will be worse when I have work both for Mr. Goldwyn and Mr. Lehr. Everybody is so temperamental and childish in this business, that in order to get on I suppose I shall have to adopt an attitude of complete indifference and develop a tough hide so that all their words will roll off and leave me entirely unaffected.

Have you seen "The Dark Angel" in New York? We have just bought the play for Colman and I've just finished typing it. I think it's splendid and am very enthused about it. If you ever see it, will you let me know what you think about it?

Everything is hustling and bustling on the lot. Frank Lloyd's new picture "Winds of Chance" is in production and the stage is set right outside my office. The scenes are supposed to be in Alaska, so it is rather funny to see the extras in big heavy fur coats and hats in this climate. There are big, sinister looking men with long beards and girls in old fashioned clothes—bright colors and just now they are staging the interior of a typical Alaska dance hall and everybody is shouting and having a hilarious time.

On the other stage there is a society drama going on and a big interior of a society dance. Nita Naldi has just come off the set—she is wearing a flame colored evening gown, cut V to the waist in the back. She is gorgeous. Her beauty just takes your breath away—but what an awakening when she talks—so vulgar and loud. Corrine Griffith is working on the same set and she is very haughty and disdainful. She looks at no one but her dogs and is generally disliked by all. It's rather queer to see so many people mingling together in totally different costumes—men in evening clothes, canes, spats, high silk hats with grizzly bearded men in plaid shirts, boots and sombreros.

I haven't time to write more to you just now but will in a few days. Remember me to all the folks.

As ever, Valeria

APRIL 8, 1925

Dear Irma,

I've been receiving more papers from you, but no letter. Of course, I appreciate the papers, but I'd like a little letter from you too.

Haven't been fired yet, but bawled out a number of times, but I don't mind it because I'm tremendously enthusiastic about my work.

Frances Marion has just finished the Stella Dallas script and to my mind it's going to be one of the biggest pictures of the year, especially considering that Henry King is going to direct it. I'm quite friendly with Mr. King's assistant director, Jimmy Dugan. He likes Italians very much and wants me to teach him how to speak Italian because King may do a picture in Italy again. I'm trying to work in so that if they do go, I may have a chance of going too.

I'm enclosing a print from our last picture "His Supreme Moment" because I want to call your attention to the fact that the background in this film is not natural, but a painted one. Don't you think it's good? "His Supreme Moment" opens at the Strand around April 12th and if you can see it, I wish you would and then let me have your opinion.

I'm also enclosing some "stills" of Lewis Stone that I thought you might like to see and a picture of Ronald Colman.

A friend of mine, Ruth Trolander, who worked in Mr. Loeb's office, is now working on the lot with me as Joseph Schenck's secretary. She is getting $60 a week to start. If Mr. Goldwyn finds me satisfactory that is what I expect to get in a short time. The studios pay big salaries to their girls but you certainly earn it. It's no simple matter working for people who are as nervous and temperamental as movie people are.

Last night when I called for Ruth at Mr. Schenck's office,* I met Mr. W. R. Hearst. I didn't know him by sight and had quite a novel introduction. I came rushing through the door with much speed and he was coming out from an inner door and we collided. If he had been about 4 feet shorter than he is, I might have knocked him over. We both laughed and I said some fool thing—don't recall what it was. While I was waiting for Ruth, he came back then was introduced to me and I surely was surprised when I found out who he was. He and Schenck are planning to erect the largest broadcasting stations in the country—one in California, one in Chicago, and one in New York I believe. Mr. Hearst is quite tall, but he has such a small voice that you are quite surprised when he opens his mouth.

I saw Constance Talmadge today having her hair dried on the porch right next to my office. I was so surprised to see she had blonde hair. Also met Ben Lyon who is so good looking that one can't help but like him.

Went horseback riding in Beverly Hills with our landlord and his son. He belongs to the L.A. Riding Academy and has a season ticket so that we can go every Sunday if we want to. I was sore for about 2

*Joe Schenck had just been named head of United Artists, the company formed by Mary Pickford, Doug Fairbanks, Charles Chaplin, and D. W. Griffith in 1919. Before that, Schenck was a successful film producer for his wife, Norma Talmadge, his sister-in-law, Constance Talmadge, and their sister Natalie's husband, Buster Keaton.

weeks after but I suppose if I keep it up I'll learn how to ride without these minor inconveniences.

Vilma Banky has arrived and I like her very much. With good management, she ought to be a success. She can't speak English so most of our conversation is by gestures and a word here and there.

I'm so happy to be here at the studio that I just wish that all my friends were here too. I like the atmosphere and the hustle and bustle of this life. Everybody but my boss is so nice and friendly—so different from a regular business office. No one but the art director, Mr. Anton Grot, has gotten too friendly as yet. Mr. Grot tried once to kiss me but my guess is that he won't try that again.

I'm having a white flannel ensemble made—no fur on the coat and I'm getting a white sport hat to go with it. I've just gotten my blue suit from the tailors and it looks quite well. I wear a boy's shirt with a bright orange tie and I have a pretty orange hat. With my white suit I'll have four outfits—not counting sweaters and skirts and I hope Mr. Goldwyn will be satisfied with my appearance. I was over to Ruth's just now and I took a picture of Norma Talmadge to send you. We also stopped by one of the stages and . . . [end of letter]

[Written on Samuel Goldwyn stationery with following note at top:]

Don't think I'm using the company's paper for personal use—these letter heads have been scrapped, so I have no scruples about using it.

APRIL 23, 1925
Dear Irma,

Your lovely long letter received. You have been a tremendous help to me by sending the clippings of theatrical news. The write up you sent me of "His Supreme Moment" was the first to reach the studio and Mr. Lehr was tickled to read it. He immediately called up Frances Marion and read it to her. They discussed Jane Winton and Mr. Lehr told me that Frances Marion as well as himself didn't approve of her, but Mr. Fitzmaurice wanted her, so of course they had to accede to the director's wishes. On the whole I think it's good criticism and it ought to make money for Mr. Goldwyn.

Today Ronald Colman and Constance Talmadge started on a new picture. I believe it will be called "The Twins." I was on the stage watching them "shoot" a scene and was quite thrilled watching them both act. Ronald is certainly good looking and he's so modest about it that one can't help but like him. Ronald doesn't like Constance at all and I'm wondering if he'll be able to make love to her sincerely. There is no doubt that at some time or other he'll be called upon to do it, as movies are never made without (as they call it here) "heart interest."

No doubt by this time you know that Mr. Goldwyn has married Miss Frances Howard. In a way I'm glad because it might make him just a little more gentle and considerate of his secretary. We have just telephoned Mr. Goldwyn that we are going to give him a dinner on his arrival and these are the distinguished guests which I am inviting: Mary Pickford, Douglas Fairbanks, Joseph Schenck, Norma Talmadge, Constance Talmadge, Charlie Chaplin, Frances Marion and her husband Fred Thomson, Ronald Colman and Vilma Banky. I was also to invite Marion Davies, but she has just left Los Angeles.

Marion Davies had quite a blow out last week for the opening of her new picture "Zander the Great". Everybody who is somebody in the movie industry was there. The papers made an awful splash about it and it was one of the gala events of the year. Mr. Hearst wasn't there for the opening, but I know that he personally arranged the whole affair with Mr. Schenck and then left for New York (I think it's New York, but not certain) the day before the opening. While the picture is good, it is by no means a marvelous production and it certainly didn't warrant the fuss that was made at the opening. I heard Mr. Lehr discussing the matter with Frances [Marion, screenwriter of *Zander the Great*] over the telephone and this is what he said: "Of course, Daddy had to show off his little girl and there's nothing too good for her. Daddy wants everybody to think his little girl is wonderful and he'll spare no expense to convince them." I went to see the picture last night and I certainly didn't think much of it. I suppose it was due to the fact that I had seen it on the stage with Alice Brady.

Charlie Chaplin has just chartered Hearst's yacht for his wife, who is expecting a child very soon. I don't know just what the idea is of going away for the event, but I presume there must be some reason for it which I don't know.

We are starting to cast our next picture, "Stella Dallas" and are having quite a time deciding who will play Stella. That is the most important role in the picture and we must be careful to select an exceptionally good actress. If Stella is miscast, the picture will be ruined. I can hardly wait until the picture is finished because I think it's going to be one of the best pictures in years.

I've had quite some time off last week, almost every afternoon, because my manager expects I will be very busy when Mr. Goldwyn gets back and he wants me to feel fit. That's very considerate of him, don't you think so?

I haven't read much lately, just some of Edna St. Vincent Millay's poems and Shaw's "Pygmalion," "Overruled" and "Androcles and the Lion." We are not considering any new material in the office just now because we will be busy for the next six months on the material we have on hand.

I went to see Mary Boland in "Meet the Wife." This played on Broadway last year and has only just reached Los Angeles. It's very clever and I enjoyed it very much. Also saw "Dark Angel" played by a second rate company which was not so good. I manage to go to the movies once a week, but I don't go necessarily for entertainment. I make it my business to go to see a picture if there is something outstanding in it, that is, if it is exceptionally well directed or the photography is good, or the continuity is good, or if the acting of some new player is outstanding, etc. I've been to two concerts, one by Chaliapin and one of Tito Schipa. I was so thrilled to hear Schipa, especially when he sang Italian songs. It's so long since I've heard the Italian language that I just cried when I heard him sing. He has a wonderful voice, and it's a long time since I've been moved as I was that night.

Easter Sunday I went to Catalina with Florence and Nancy. Irma, you should have seen the island. It was a mass of flowers. The beauty of it, together with the memory of my first visit there with you, made me supremely happy and I was content to just look. I couldn't even talk.

Last Saturday I was driving through the mountains near Los Angeles and through orange groves. The groves are now in blossom and the odor is almost sickening it is so strong. You can usually smell a grove about a mile before you get to it. Just as soon as I can get into town I'm going to send you a box of orange blossoms, and I hope they will retain some of their odor by the time you receive them.

I'm glad to hear that you are well, and I trust Ida's baby will be over the worst of her whooping cough. I want to again thank you for your kindness and thoughtfulness in sending me that most interesting page of all New York papers and hope it doesn't give you too much trouble to send it on to me as you have been doing.

With kindest regards to all, I am

As ever, Valeria

APRIL 27, 1925

I neglected to post my letter of April 23 so I am amplifying it with this note. I just received your letter today and you ask me how I like my boss. Coincidentally, today was the first time I have seen him. He came in about 4, was introduced to him and outside of getting two numbers for him, had nothing to do with him. In about a week, I'll be able to let you know how things develop. Be quite sure that I won't get thin over my job. I am here on a lark and I'm not taking anything seriously.

I've been introduced to a stockbroker and he has induced me to buy some Sinclair Oil stock. I've only invested $180 and thought I could risk that much. Of course this fellow is quite a good friend of mine and he seems to think it's a very good buy, so I feel confident that I haven't done anything foolish. I'm also buying a car—haven't decided what kind—excepting that it will be a Ford. I'm already seeing myself crossing the country in it. I'd just love to do that with about 2 other girls. You can tell Spring is here. I do get the wandering fever so badly, don't you? Here's one of Edna St. Vincent Millay's poems called "Travel"

The railroad track is miles away,
And the day is loud with voices speaking,
Yet there isn't a train goes by all day
But I hear its whistle shrieking.

All night there isn't a train goes by
Though the night is still for sleep and dreaming,
But I see its cinders red on the sky,
And hear its engine steaming.

My heart is warm with the friends I make,
And better friends I'll not be knowing
Yet there isn't a train I wouldn't take
No matter where it's going.

After working at the studio for nearly three months as his private secretary, Valeria finally met Sam Goldwyn. He had left for Europe in January, just weeks before Valeria was hired. Europe was an important market for American films, and Goldwyn visited with his family in between his meetings in various capital cities. In Budapest he saw a photograph of a strikingly beautiful young woman and, before leaving the next day, managed to meet the twenty-seven-year-old he would call "Banky Vilma" or just "Wilma." The thought that films would not always be silent had hardly occurred to Sam or to anyone else in early 1925, and therefore speaking English was not a prerequisite to film stardom in America. (At that moment Lars Hanson, who spoke only Swedish, was preparing to star opposite Lillian Gish in MGM's *The Scarlet Letter;* Louis B. Mayer had signed him the year before in Berlin, along with the director Mauritz Stiller and the actress Greta Gustafson who changed her last name to Garbo.)

Vilma Banky was sent on ahead of Sam, via Paris, to be properly coutured and prepared for the massive publicity campaign he envisioned for his new star. He already had her first film planned, *The Dark Angel*, costarring Ronald Colman.

Sam reunited with Vilma in New York and spent time "squiring" her around town. On one of those see-and-be-seen evenings, Sam and Vilma joined several hundred other guests at the publisher Condé Nast's thirty-room penthouse, and Sam was smitten on sight when he spotted the twenty-one-year-old redheaded actress Frances Howard. The very next day, Sam put Vilma on the train for Hollywood, took Frances to dinner, and proposed marriage.

The Omaha-born Frances had been raised in Catholic boarding schools until her once-flush father was victimized by his own brothers' embezzling of the family company. Her father responded by turning to liquor and died shortly thereafter, leaving his wife, Bonnie, who had known only wealth and a comfortable lifestyle, distraught and unable to cope. She moved the fourteen-year-old Frances and her three younger children to Manhattan, where Frances took to the stage and assumed financial responsibility for her entire family. By most accounts, she was not much of an actress, but so breathtaking to look at, she worked consistently. Frances was seventeen and preparing for a featured role in a Rochester, New York, road show when she met the twenty-year-old stage manager, soon to be director, George Cukor. Even then, Cukor was struck by what he called her "soignée" aura, and the two quickly realized they were genuinely in love. They discussed marriage, and Cukor believed they might make a success of it because Frances was "never highly sexed," but the fact was he was gay and knew better. Instead, they remained close friends, so it was natural that Frances turned to George for his opinion when Sam Goldwyn persisted and proposed again on their second date the next night.

While Frances later said, "Right off the bat, I thought to myself, 'Why not?'" she had to be a bit surprised when Cukor, after a moment's pause, affirmed her conclusion, bluntly telling her, "Marry him, Frances. You'll never get a better part."

He had no idea how right he was. Sam Goldwyn had cast Frances in the role of his wife: the beautiful gentile, an apparently well-bred and cultured stunner whose mother was the same age as Sam. He was at the point in his career that he needed a wife, and here was the woman he wanted on his arm. Pragmatic, looking for security, and — consciously or not — anxious to get away from her clinging yet overbearing mother (who openly called Jews "Christ killers" or "Orientals"), Frances accepted Goldwyn's proposal as the long-term contract it was.

Frances Howard and Sam Goldwyn were married on April 23, 1925, a month to the day after their first meeting. They took a limousine across the river to Jersey City's city hall (sidestepping the ban Valeria noted on his remarrying in New York). Sam's former partner Edgar Selwyn was his best man; Frances's mother and George Cukor represented her family. After a small reception for fewer than two dozen friends at the Ritz, Sam and his bride stopped by his New York office and then headed for the station to catch the train for California.

Upon their arrival in Los Angeles, Sam took Frances to the home he had leased at the corner of Hollywood Boulevard and Camino Palmero and proceeded to leave her there while he went to his studio. Then, that very evening, they were off to the home of Richard Rowland, head of First National Studios, for the dinner Valeria and Abe Lehr had planned. In addition to the guests Valeria names, Pola Negri, John Gilbert, Florence Vidor, and Ernst Lubitsch were in attendance.

Frances didn't have time to be awed by the stars she met at the "welcome home" dinner. When she overheard a man dismissively referring to "some wives," she felt she had been doused with a bucket of cold water. At that moment she realized now she was just a "wife" in a town where business was all that mattered. Yet, practical to the core, Frances determined to take on that role with the same ambition and professionalism that had helped her persevere on the stage. And she succeeded. Irene Selznick claimed, "Sam, who couldn't get along with anyone, could not, in my opinion, have gotten along without her. On the whole, Frances did the best job of wifehood in Hollywood."

With assistance from Frances Marion and Peg Talmadge, mother of actresses Constance and Norma, Frances Goldwyn learned to be a superb hostess, and Sam glowed in his casting coup. In the process, she became the one partner he could work with, and she added immeasurably to his success. Just as she smoothed his edges with much of Hollywood, Frances helped Valeria to understand Sam and be patient with him.

When Valeria expressed hope that having a wife might make Sam "just a little more gentle and considerate of his secretary," she was half right. Sam was and would always be incorrigible in his relationships, with equals as well as underlings, but Frances became his constant advocate. She brought Valeria gifts and assured her of how much Sam appreciated his secretary, making the thoughtful gestures that would never occur to Sam.

Sam himself was a bit startling to Valeria. She had been forewarned about his gruffness as well as his "skirt chasing"; she was used to Lawrence Langner, an always polite and communicative boss, and she found Goldwyn's literally ignoring her difficult to comprehend, let alone adjust to. She would soon learn that he talked to her only when something was wrong and grew to interpret his silence as good news.

Just the month before, the *New Yorker* had described Sam's style in a profile: "To hear him speak is a shock. He shouts in a vocabulary of ten words — words used by a prize fighter who has gone into the cloak and suit business and upon whose modular tones an expressman has let fall a half ton case of goods. If after an interview you are a bit raw, he won't know it." Goldwyn's obliviousness to those around him soon hit his new secretary like that "half ton case" and, quite naturally, it was difficult not to take it personally.

....

MAY 6, 1925

Dear Irma,

I'm dropping you a hurried letter in the office—it's about 6:15 and I have nothing to do, but I must wait until Mr. Lehr gets through talking with Mr. Beaudine (Mary Pickford's director) before I can go home.

Well, Mr. Goldwyn hasn't "jumped down my throat" yet. I don't particularly like him, but I don't think he's any worse than the others.

I'm kept terribly busy because I have to keep track of practically everything in the office and since we are starting 3 pictures, it means work to do it. Mr. Henry King hasn't a secretary yet, and I have to do work for him as well as do little personal things for Ronald Colman.

I have to write nearly all of Mr. Goldwyn's letters because he certainly doesn't know anything about grammar. He signs all the letters I write for him and so far hasn't made any comments so I presume they suit him.

If I work here until August, I believe I shall be able to take about 3 weeks vacation. If I do, you'll see me because I'll take a trip east with Mr. Goldwyn who expects to leave then too.

My work is really hard. I have to talk, talk, talk all day long. People are constantly wanting to see Mr. Goldwyn about getting into pictures or they have "a marvelous story" that they can't mail to the office, but must see Mr. Goldwyn personally about it. I have to smooth things over and keep them away. Just recently I had a French actor who just kept begging me to see Mr. Goldwyn. I finally did manage to get him an appointment with Mr. Dugan and when I told him about it, he nearly fell on his knees thanking me. Sir Henry McGriran [?] who is the "Schwab" of England has been Mr. Goldwyn's guest for 3 days and I've had a lot of work for him. Can you imagine it, he's worth millions and when he left he not even as much as left a box of candy for me.

Well, the conference is over so I'll close my letter because I'm anxious to get home. The 3 of us girls have fellows coming to the house tonight. My friend is a Mr. Colgrove who is a struggling lawyer—just starting.

Love to all, Valeria

MAY 20, 1925

Dear Irma

I have a few spare moments in the office today—therefore I'm writing to you. I'm so happy because I have an idea Mr. Goldwyn likes me. Mrs. Goldwyn told me that Mr. Goldwyn thought I was wonderful. Of course she might be saying this only to make me feel good, but if she is, it certainly did change my mental attitude towards my work. I like it ever so much better and in view of this I feel happier. Mrs. Goldwyn is so nice to me—she comes to the studio almost every morning and chats with me.

I'm tremendously busy—it seems I have to write letters for everybody. We have another girl in the outside office, but nobody gives her work because she is rather stupid. Mr. Henry King hands me his mail and says "Here, answer it—I don't care what you say, so long as you're polite in declining everything."

Most of the letters are from actresses looking for jobs—so I just write a lot of blarney and sign his name to them. I do this for his assistant director Mr. Dugan as well and of course for my own boss, Mr. Goldwyn. I don't mind doing this because I can say what I like and they don't want to see my letters. Sometimes when some of the actresses call up and they are very persistent about seeing either Mr. Goldwyn or Mr. King, I tell them to call and see me and I take their photographs, experiences and all other data and enter on my records and then I tell them that just as soon as I can arrange an appointment with Mr. Goldwyn or Mr. King, I'll be glad to let them know. This invariably pleases them and they go away and leave me alone for a while.

Next week, Mr. King will have a secretary of his own and then I'll be relieved of some work. By the way, I already have had an offer to work in Mr. Schenck's office as secretary to his assistant. My salary would be the same as here, that is, $40 a week, but I turned it down because I think I'll be able to get much more if I stick it out here.

I'm getting to know quite a lot of people and Mr. Dugan has already invited me to a little studio gathering. It wasn't a party exactly, but they had some scotch, so we had a few highballs and everybody was quite funny. Dugan is awfully friendly towards me, but I don't want to encourage him because I know he's married and of course I don't want to be involved in any affair with a married man. He tried to tell me that there wouldn't be any harm in his taking me out occasionally but I sternly refused to listen to him.

I told him that with all the extra girls running after him ready to give themselves up to him for the sake of a little part in some picture, why should he want to take me out when he knew I wasn't a good sport. This is what he said:

"Listen here. I've had enough of them—the very sight of girls of that sort repulse me. If I take a girl out I want one that I know I can talk to and don't have to make love to. I couldn't do that with those girls, but I can with you, because I know that you're not like them. I understand girls pretty well and I know you're good and haven't been out with a lot of men. That's why I want to take you."

Of course his saying this didn't change my mind, although I must confess I'd like to go to some wild Hollywood party just to see what it's like and if they are as bad as they are pictured.

I played golf last Sunday—Nancy and I met two fellows at the links and they were very nice to us. I really don't know what I should have done if I hadn't met someone to show me how to play, because it was the first time I had ever been on a golf course. I was told I did very well and am quite enthusiastic about the game. Nancy and I are going again this Sunday.

Next Wednesday night I'm going horseback riding with a girl who is an art student here in Los Angeles. Nancy met her down at San Juan Capistrano at the mission. (Do you remember that beautiful spot—that lovely flower garden in the patio—and the artist we saw painting the mission?) Her name is Mary and she is so interesting. We are all going riding, that is Nancy, Florence, Mary and I and I'm looking forward to it with great pleasure.

I've just finished a book by May Sinclair called "Arnold Waterlow". It's quite interesting, but not as good as some of her other books. Jane Cowl has just reached Los Angeles in "Romeo and Juliet" and I went to see it again. I had already seen it in New York over a year ago, but I enjoyed it nevertheless. That's about all I've done in the way of "culture" for the last 3 weeks. I'm getting bad—but you see I work until pretty late every night so that when I get home I just don't feel like reading or going to shows.

I had lunch at the studio with Rudolph Valentino's publicity man today and he told me all about Rudolph—what a wonderful chap he is, can speak 4 languages—Italian, French, Spanish and English. He's quite a mechanic too and in his spare time he usually dons overalls and works on his car. He's very well read too and he's about the most cultured of all the movie stars. His wife is very intellectual too, and they get along splendidly. It makes me feel good to hear all this about a "wop" because you know how most of them are spoken of very unkindly.

I was watching a set with Viola Dana ("Winds of Chance" is the name of the picture) and Viola was supposed to be dying. I saw them shoot her death bed scene and then she sat up and said in a very tough voice: "Hey, Mame" (that's her maid) "Gimme a cigarette."

She is certainly hard, and you can see it in her face. However, most of the people at the studio like her because she is a good sport and spends her money freely.

My boss has just come in, so I must quit. Give my love to all.

Valeria

JUNE 6, 1925
Dear Irma,

I'm stuck in the office waiting for a phone call from Sid Grauman (owner of all the big theaters in Los Angeles, also the Egyptian Theater in Hollywood) and have nothing to do.

I've had a perfectly wonderful week. This was convention week of the Shriners and the city was simply wild with excitement. It was gayly decorated and there was a spirit of revelry and joy in the atmosphere that made one absolutely gay and happy. I went to dances in nearly all the hotels and was out nearly every night. Met some very nice fellows from Minneapolis and from Texas.

Last night the motion picture industry gave an Electrical Pageant which was the most beautiful thing I have ever seen. Magnificent floats all lighted in stunning effects and all the stars in Hollywood were there. The parade entered the Coliseum which holds 100,000 people (it's something like the Stadium at Columbia College—only much larger) at 9 o'clock and wasn't over until 1 in the morning. My boss was in the first car with Mr. and Mrs. Harold Lloyd and Norma Talmadge. By the way I had to pull some strings to get him there, but I succeeded so he was quite pleased with me. In the second car was Mrs. Goldwyn, Douglas Fairbanks and Rudolph Valentino and so on down the line. You should have seen all the cowboys and Indians too—it was so thrilling—all the star cowboys such as Hoot Gibson, Jack Hoxie, William Desmond, W. S. Hart with all their regalia were there. I was so thrilled because it was a magnificent sight to see so many people all seated in one place—there was a big moon shining too—right in the middle of the bowl. There were more than 100,000 people outside of the Coliseum who couldn't get in, and cars were parked for blocks and blocks around the place. I don't think I have ever seen so many cars in my life before. I had wonderful seats too—reserved in the front line right near the reviewing stand.

One day of the week it rained all day and the Shriners sure did razz the Californians. Most of the natives of course couldn't understand why it should rain at this time of year, as it is very unusual—the

Shriners immediately made up songs something like this: "It hasn't rained for forty years—but it rained like hell today" and then ended up by shouting "VERY unusual". One of the Shriners was walking along the street and every man that came along he'd go up to him and say "Oh, just a little dust on you, it's been so dry, let me brush it off." Others were standing on the policemen's boxes in the middle of the streets in their bathing suits with fishing rods and others were walking around in little pink and blue parasols. Californians sure did get razzed, but it created lots of fun so they took it good-naturedly.

We're awfully busy in the office. The cast for "Stella Dallas" is nearly completed. Belle Bennett will play Stella; Alice Joyce, Mrs. Morrison; Ronald Colman, Mr. Morrison; Douglas Fairbanks Jr. will play Laurel's sweetheart and Lois Moran (that's the 16-year-old girl Mr. Goldwyn brought from Paris) will play Laurel; the riding master Ed Munn will be played by Jean Hersholt. As for "The Dark Angel", so far we have only Vilma Banky and Ronald Colman for it. We've just finished the scripts of both plays and we have two art directors sketching the sets and the wardrobe is being made for the leading players.

I like my work ever so much better than I did at first. Mrs. Goldwyn is so nice to me—this morning she asked me if I didn't think Mr. Goldwyn was queer. She said "I think it's terrible the way he comes in in the morning and doesn't even say 'Good Morning' to you." I told her that I didn't mind it because I was quite used to eccentric people and understood them quite a bit. If Mrs. Goldwyn likes me and Mr. Goldwyn is also pleased, I see where I'm going to strike them for a ten dollar raise in about two months. I can't very well ask for more now, because in the next ten weeks we'll be spending about $600,000 on the new pictures and it would be rather an inopportune time to ask for it. However—if (that little "if" must be used here) Stella Dallas is successful I see where I shall be sitting pretty because Mr. Goldwyn is negotiating to join the United Artists (which consists of Mary Pickford, Douglas Fairbanks, Norma Talmadge and Rudolf Valentino) and they won't take him unless "Stella Dallas" proves a sensation. Therefore if Mr. Goldwyn eventually becomes a member of the United Artists and I'm his secretary, why naturally I'll get a big salary. I imagine something like $75 per week. Won't that be great? I'm just hoping and praying for his sake as well as mine that it will be a success. Henry King is very enthusiastic about it too, because Mr. Goldwyn intends signing him up and the next picture he'll make may be "The Garden of Allah" and "Romeo and Juliet." I hope they do make "Romeo and Juliet" and decide to go to Italy in order to get correct atmosphere and as I know some Italian I imagine they ought to want to send me with Mr. King. Do you know Irma, I just think of this continually I have my heart so set on it—that some day I will go to Italy to work for the studio and have my transportation paid and have my heart's desire. I had my heart set on going to California—I dreamed of it until it came true—when I was in California I had my heart set on working in one of the studios and I dreamed about it and it came true. I wonder if this dream will come true? However, if it doesn't I at least enjoyed the dreaming which is better than no dreams at all.

Write to me soon and tell me all about yourself and your family. I do so love to hear from you.

As Ever,

I have been receiving papers from you—thanks so much—they are a treat. At heart I'm an easterner yet. How is West New York—

improving? Real estate still high? My Sinclair stock is still up—if I sell now will make about $100, am still holding on to it.

JUNE 10, 1925

Dear Irma,

I received your very interesting letter last night. I'm replying promptly because fortunately or unfortunately, which ever it may be, my boss is home sick today and consequently I have very little to do. Mr. Lehr, my other boss, has gone home early in order to be able to read the last script of "Stella Dallas" without disturbance so I'm here alone.

I'm sending you under separate cover the first draft of the "Stella Dallas" script or continuity as written by Frances Marion. This has been revised quite a bit, but it will give you an idea of how things are done. After the script is finally finished, then work begins on a picture. First of all a copy is handed over to the designer who makes a "wardrobe continuity" and makes all the clothes to fit the leading players. A copy is also given to the art director who makes designs of all the scenes as described in the continuity. The designs for all the clothes and sets must be O.K.ed by Mr. King and Mr. Goldwyn. This is quite a big job and requires about two weeks to do.

After the sets have been designed, then the architect has to start building the sets so that they will be ready when Mr. King starts shooting. On some of the exterior scenes, the company will have to go to Monterey and Del Monte for location because we have no rivers in Southern California and as you will see from the script some of the scenes call for a river. Mr. King spent about three days with

Mr. Dugan around San Francisco looking for locations and these have all been found.

I'm training you so that if you ever decide to come to California to live and want to work in a studio you'll have an idea of what it's all about. I'm also sending you a back number of one of our casting directories. While the script is being done, the cast is usually picked out and these books are used to get the players for the smaller parts.

What you tell me of your new outfit makes me think you must have surely made a hit with the man your cousin Lena introduced you to. If you didn't there must be something wrong with the man or you didn't try hard enough, without letting him know you were trying—do you understand what I mean? I'm anxious to know how this affair develops. If your friend is romantic, I can reassure you that there is no place so full of romances as California, especially Hollywood—although the Hollywood kind of romance is not quite to my liking—it reeks too much of the flesh—not enough of the imagination and spirit. However, it's my guess most men like the Hollywood kind.

I haven't gone out with Dugan and don't think I ever will. He's been ever so nice to me and although every time I pass his room he wants me to take a drink with him, he hasn't annoyed me in any way. What I'd like to know is how I'm expected to be able to work and drink at the same time. The men seem to be able to do it, and even the girls, but I can't. One night one of the men gave me a drink about five and since I thought I would be soon going home, it wouldn't interfere with my work (you know one must be a little sociable with their co-workers—If I didn't, I'd get a pretty bad reputation and I wouldn't be able to get anyone to do anything for me. In view of my position I have to give a lot of orders to everybody from Mr. Goldwyn and if I'm on good terms with everybody I can get better results).

Well, to drift back to my original story, I took the drink and that evening Mr. Goldwyn decided to stay in the office until about 6:30 and believe me, my fingers went all over the keyboard and it seemed to me I had more than ten fingers or there were twice as many keys. It's a good thing I had only one drink so that I was able to manage, but can you imagine if I had had more what would have happened?

Since then, I have absolutely refused to drink at work, as I don't like it so much that I'd want to risk losing my job through it. Since we have so much to do, the assistant directors and the other men here at the studio as well as myself have been provided with a car and chauffeur (the car is a Ford) who runs errands for us and takes us where we want to go. McCready (that's our man's name) takes me home every night. This is quite a help.

I was horseback riding last Sunday with four other girls in Griffith Park and had a terrible experience. My horse ran off with me and I couldn't stop him. I held on for dear life and thought I'd faint any moment. After riding wildly for about a mile, I heard another horse come galloping after me and someone was shouting instructions as to what I should do. I tried to keep cool and do as I was told and finally succeeded in stopping the horse. My hands are all torn from holding on to the reins and the skin on my legs is rubbed off from clinging to the horse so tightly. I'm all bunged up and can thank my lucky star that I didn't fall off or lose my head. I swore if I ever got off that horse alive I'd never go on another.

The man who came after me was very nice to me and I certainly don't know what I would have done if he hadn't been behind me, because I was somewhere in the Hollywood Hills, but I didn't know where—I was cut off from everybody so that if he hadn't been there I don't know how I could have gotten back. He took hold of my horse and we went back through beautiful country (I hadn't seen it of course on my wild ride) and he was telling me all about horses and how to ride. When we got near the stable I met one of the girls of our crowd and she immediately dismissed him and said she would take care of me. I'm so sorry I didn't speak up and ask him to come over to the stable with me because I would have liked to have known him better. As it is I don't know his name and the only way I can meet him again I suppose is by going riding. Therefore, I think I shall go riding again because I really would like to meet him.

The climate now is about the same as it was when you were here. There is very little difference. In the morning and especially at night you really need a heavy coat, but during the day it's warm, although not uncomfortably so.

I went to a preview of a picture last night. Mr. Lehr couldn't go so he gave me his tickets. The picture was one taken on the lot so that I had seen most of the sets shot when I first came to the studio. I'd like you to see the picture when it comes out because there are some Venetian carnival scenes (taken on the lot) which really are good. Most people will think they were actually taken in Venice. Also the desert and street scenes were all built on the lot. The name of the picture is "The Woman who Lied" with Lewis Stone, Virginia Valli and Nita Naldi. The picture is not so good, but the sets are worthwhile seeing.

I've been a little lonesome this week and have quite a longing to see all my old friends. I'm looking forward to coming East in the fall and only hope that I will be given time off without losing my job.

If I manage to come, I'll take about 3 weeks so that I will be home only about 8 days. In those eight days I want to do a lot of shopping and take in some shows so that I'll be pretty busy. I'd be delighted to have you arrange so that you won't be away when I come because it would be quite tragic so far as I am concerned if after coming all that distance I were not to see you.

Give my best to all your folks and I want to again thank you for the papers which I keep on getting from you.

Valeria

JUNE 26, 1925

Dear Irma,

I've had a hectic morning—but thank the Lord my Boss went to the beach with his wife at 1:30 so that I have very little to do this afternoon. Furthermore, both companies are on the lot shooting, so that the studio is more or less deserted. Tonight is the Charlie Chaplin "Gold Rush" premier at the Grauman's Egyptian Theater and after the show Mr. Goldwyn is giving a party at his home for Charlie. Mrs. Goldman and I invited the guests several days ago but this morning Mr. Goldwyn had me call them all up and make sure they were coming. These are some of the guests: Elinor Glyn, Fred Niblo (director of Ben Hur), Mr. Fitzmaurice, Florence Vidor, Marion Davies, Mr. Hearst, Louella Parsons, Mr. and Mrs. King, John Barrymore, Buster Keaton, Norma and Constance Talmadge, Gloria Swanson and her Marquis, Sid Grauman, Mary Pickford and Douglas Fairbanks, and a number of other people you wouldn't know. In addition to having to do this, my boss has taken me so into his confidence that he entrusted me with the responsibility of getting the booze for the party. I got names of nearly all of the reliable bootleggers in town and after much discussion and fuss I got the right kind of stuff (at the right price) and Mr. Goldwyn was tickled. Not only was he pleased, but so was the bootlegger, because I gave him an order for about $300 worth of stuff and paid him cash on the spot. He is now a friend of mine, and I can get any thing from him at a real low price. It's too bad I can't take advantage of it.

....

Basil Woon, a chronicler of the times, noted that Los Angeles was largely dependent on bootleggers, for unlike other major American cities, it had relatively few speakeasies. He claimed this was "because the Los Angeles resident has the bootlegger habit — he is trained to drink at home or in the home of his friends — and partly because it is easier to call a 'legger than to get the car out and travel miles to the nearest speak." Hundreds of bootleggers flourished in Hollywood during Prohibition, stocked with liquor that was either made locally or brought in from boats anchored in the nearby harbor. Although parties like the one Valeria was stocking were common, there was still a mystique to dealing with a bootlegger. Other, more serious drinkers, depended upon other means. The director George Hill had a prescription for a pint of liquor a day from his doctor, and his assistant director Joe Newman remembered one of his duties was a 4 o'clock run to the pharmacy every afternoon to pick up Hill's liquor. Pathé president J. J. Murdock bought a Beverly Hills home with a still and a large bar installed in the basement, protected by steel doors that could be closed with the flip of a switch from upstairs in case the authorities made an unexpected appearance. And just before Prohibition was to go into effect,

Charlotte Pickford, Mary's mother, bought the contents of a liquor store and had it all moved into her basement.

I'm afraid our happy little home is going to be broken up. Flo is leaving Saturday for home and Nancy is taking a vacation—as for myself—I haven't made any plans yet. I'm relying on something to turn up at the last minute. In view of this I think you had better address my mail to the studio as follows:

> c/o Samuel Goldwyn
> United Studios
> 5341 Melrose Avenue
> Hollywood, Calif.

The three of us are planning to get together again in the fall, as we certainly got along splendidly and our home life was ideal.

You ought to see Ronald Colman in his British uniform as he appears in "Dark Angel." He is a stunner. My heart skips a beat every time he talks to me. As for Vilma—she is adorable. I know she is going to make a tremendous hit. By the way, Rudolph Valentino is trying to get her for his leading lady in his next picture.

I'm going to tell you something about Belle Bennett who is going to play Stella which is very sad. When Belle was given the part of Stella, it was of course the climax of her career. She had never had a big part in pictures and was longing to do Stella. I'm enclosing a letter she wrote to Mr. Lehr long before the company had started to cast the picture which will indicate how anxious she was to play the part. However, neither Mr. King nor Mr. Goldwyn gave her a thought and didn't consider her at all. After making tests of a number of well known actresses which didn't turn out satisfactory, they found themselves stumped and as a last resort they decided to give Belle a test. As you know, she succeeded and the part was given to her. We decided to start right away but found out Belle couldn't come to the studio because it so happened that her 15-year-old brother was deathly ill and she had to be at his bedside constantly. This went on for about three weeks and finally last Wednesday the boy died. The boy died in the morning and in the afternoon Belle had to come to the studio in order to get a fitting for one of her dresses she had to wear in the picture—and I was in tears when I saw her. The expression in her face is one that I shall never forget as long as I live—it was just stark tragedy. The boy was buried on Saturday and she left with the company on location in the afternoon. That same day, a personal friend of hers came to the studio and I of course asked him for details regarding the boy. To my surprise I found out that this was not her brother but her son. The tragic part of it though is that for professional reasons she had brought him up as a brother and no one knew it was her son—in fact the boy died not knowing Belle was his mother. Can you imagine the grief in her heart—it must be almost unbearable. I can understand now the look in her face. She thinks the boy was taken from her as a punishment because she had denied him. He was a big strong boy, about 6 ft. and was being trained as an all around athlete by the University of California. It seemed that in a game one of the boys kicked him in the ribs—blood poisoning set in and after six weeks of horrible suffering he died. In those six weeks Belle never left him—She wanted to tell him that she was his mother—

but she was afraid that it would hurt him and decided for his own sake to let him die thinking she was his sister. It does seem like a cruel fate to have the happiest event of her career blighted by such a tragedy. It truly seems that one can never have happiness without tears.

I hope everything is O.K. with you. How is your romance progressing? Kindly give my love to all your folks.

As ever,
Valeria

This is Belle Bennett's letter: Addressed to Mr. Lehr

Knowing you are interested in "better pictures", "better parts", "better people", "better stories", for the "better company", Samuel Goldwyn, I am offering you these few bits of genuine tributes to me, which reached me through the newspapers, feeling sure you realize the value of these compliments at this day in age when the public demands dependable, clean, wholesome artists of ability for the stars of tomorrow. We must now build our foundation for a long term contract with the world and its people.

I want "Stella Dallas" more than I have ever wanted anything in my life and I believe I'm qualified for this honor. In the theater I have played many wonderful parts, but since Samuel Goldwyn first spoke to me about the character of "Stella Dallas" I have kept the book near me, reading her over and over until she crept into my heart and soul and I want to scream at the thought of losing her. I feel that she is what I have been waiting for all my life and I have built her up bit by bit until I feel sure that I have what Henry King and Samuel Goldwyn want.

I am telling you all this because of the kindly, friendly interest which you displayed in my second and last interview with you.

However, "Whatever is, is best" and if through God's infallible wisdom he should will it that I fail to gain this big opportunity for which I have been hoping and praying for, the part of "Stella", I want you to know, my kindly friend, that I shall be a "game loser", so please keep me posted, one way or the other, as the suspense has lasted since July and is most distressing.

Please believe in me, when I tell you that I shall always be grateful to you for your encouraging words and the "kiss on the brow" when my heart was breaking. My "comeback" in pictures has not been easy and you were the first to peep into my heart and analyze the fact that it was the artist in me that was crushed and hungry for recognition, and not the woman who is striving for material gain. To own and be worthy of a great part, satisfies my soul as food saves the life of a starving woman. Hence, this last effort to make a plea for "Stella Dallas".

....

While publicity blurbs for *Stella Dallas* claimed that Belle Bennett was cast "after 73 other actors had tried for the part," Henry King said that before anyone else was even considered, Frances Marion approached him and said, "I don't know if you have given any thought to the actress to play Stella, but I would suggest you consider Belle Bennett. She has just what it takes." King had seen Bennett in a play on Broadway and thought she gave "a tremendous performance," but he credited Frances Marion with having "a great talent for picking people" and for the ultimate casting of Bennett. She had appeared in Goldwyn's 1924 *Potash and Perlmutter* in Hollywood, also written by Frances, and the two had been friends ever since. Marion knew the truth about Bennett's life, but she was diplomatic when she told King that the actress "has had everything on earth happen to her. Both on stage and off, she IS Stella Dallas." When Bennett auditioned, King said "she was magnificent" and the part was hers.

Stella Dallas was a novel by Olivia Higgins Prouty, billed as an archetypical tearjerker of "mother love." Stella is a "gross, common" woman whose only truly sympathetic characteristic is her unconditional love for her child. Stella has trapped her upper-class husband, Stephen, into marriage on the rebound after a family tragedy, but when she realizes the only way her daughter will have a chance at a better life is to remove herself, Stella divorces Stephen and feigns a situation where her daughter, Laurel, will leave her and move in with Stephen and his new wife. And, just as Stella had hoped, Laurel grows into a beautiful young woman and becomes engaged to a rich, debonair young man, played by Douglas Fairbanks Jr.

The novel unfolds in flashbacks, but Frances Marion adapted the story into a straight chronologically told script, agonizing over finding that "thin line between convincing sentimentality and lachrymose melodrama." The film ends on the day of Laurel's wedding at Stephen's home. The curtains have been left open, and Laurel, exquisite in her wedding gown, uses the window as a reflecting mirror. Laurel doesn't see her, but her mother is standing outside and stays to watch, her hands holding the metal bars of the fence as if it were a jail cell. Stella is still smiling in resigned satisfaction as rain starts to fall and a policeman prods her to move along; the camera fades.

....

JULY, 1925

Dear Irma,

I'm writing to you because I have what is commonly known as the "blues" and the best way of dispelling them is by writing. Mr.

Goldwyn won't be in until late and I have nothing to do until he comes.

Last night Nancy and I went with two married couples to the beach grunion fishing. It seems that only once a year between May and July, during the full moon or three days on the wane, just a little before or after high tide and about one or two hours after the moon has risen, do these fish come in. When they start to "run" the waves carry them on the beach and all along the shore there are thousands of people, in all sorts of outfits, carrying pails, boxes, bags, cans and lamps, lights and searchlights of all kinds—and people had bathing suits on with heavy old sweaters and coats of every description. It surely was a funny sight to see all these people walking up and down the beach waiting for the fish to come in. We sat by the fire from 8:30 until about 10 when the moon began to rise and then we paraded along expecting the fish to come in any moment. Well we saw the tide come in and go out—but no fish. We stayed until 1:30 AM and then we came home—carrying all our bags, nets, lights back again. I guess I won't go grunion fishing again. We got home about 3 AM—I was cold and damp—and perhaps that accounts for my blues this morning.

Nancy and I are still in the same bungalow, but we are moving the first of August into a smaller one—in the same Court—so that any mail addressed to me at the old address will reach me, although I'll let you have my new number as soon as I know it.

I suppose you have read the news that Mr. Goldwyn has joined United Artists. Mr. King has also signed an agreement to do eight pictures for us. I'm so glad he has because I like Mr. King very much. I feel towards him somewhat like I did towards Mr. Langner. I suppose it's a sort of hero worship complex that I have for men who are really clever. According to the present schedule, Mr. King is going to do "The Garden of Allah" when he finishes "Stella Dallas." I was to be a bride's maid—but the slippers didn't fit me. He asked me if I had a pair of my own like them at home because if I did he'd send me home for them—I didn't so I lost the part.

I haven't done anything exciting for about 3 weeks—excepting one night when a friend of the family—Harold (I can't for the life of me remember his last name) took me to see some of his friends and we had an exciting game of roulette—and also some very good Muscatel. This man we went to see is a doctor and has quite a stock of real good wine. Harold was banker and won about $5.00 and I for an amateur came out 50 cents the loser which is not so bad. Harold is quite an odd individual. He knew Florence and the first time he came to the house, Florence wasn't home, but I was and he insisted on taking me out for a ride. After that he kept taking Florence out about once a month, and she would tell me that he always asked about me. When Florence left he came the next day which was Sunday and Nancy and I were home so he took the both of us out driving and then to dinner. He called me up the next day and then took me out on the following Tuesday. All week he kept in touch with me and on Sunday he called about 7 PM. I told him Nancy was at the house with her friend and if he wanted to come over he could spend an evening at home. He accepted gladly—but never showed up and I haven't heard from him since. Now what do you make of that?

Elinor Glyn was to the studio to lunch with Mr. Goldwyn.* She's

*Elinor Glyn was "a respectably salacious novelist" who wrote stories with names like *Three Weeks* and *It*, adapted to the screen for Clara Bow. At the time of her studio visit, Glyn was in her early sixties and at the top of her fame.

very eccentric—wore a pale lavender dress and hat—has a bright red wig and her face is powdered very white—her eyes are blackened and her lips are straight slits of red. She brought in a story for Mr. Fitzmaurice to read called "Her Mate." It was only in scenario form, but it was awful—regular "Elinor Glyn" stuff. I could hear Mr. Goldwyn and Fitz laughing as they were reading it. Isn't it killing to think she makes a fortune out of such stories.

This is a monstrous looking letter to be sending you—I'm writing in bits—it's now after lunch and my boss is out again so I hope I can continue until I'm finished without being interrupted.

Isn't it too bad that Santa Barbara was ruined by the earthquake?* I can never forget the beauty of it when you and I first drove through it. Remember the two old aristocrats who got off at the Arlington? The mission was wrecked but not completely and funds are already being raised in Los Angeles to restore it. I was rather thrilled when I felt the earthquake—being the first I ever experienced, but when I heard that Santa Barbara had been hit so badly, I felt really sorry. However, I guess everything will be rebuilt in no time and the quake will be forgotten. Nobody seems to worry much about them here.

The heat wave in the East is more of a topic of conversation than the quakes. So far we've had delightful weather—haven't had one sultry warm day yet. It's just cool enough to be peppy and ambitious, although I must confess I have lost all my ambition the last

*A 6.3 earthquake hit Santa Barbara, 100 miles north of Los Angeles, in the early morning of June 29, 1925, destroying much of the State Street downtown area and killing thirteen people. While most residential areas were spared serious damage beyond broken chimneys, much of the State Street downtown area was destroyed. The city would seize upon the destruction as an opportunity to strengthen building codes and design requirements that resulted in the Spanish Moorish architecture that dominates the area today.

three weeks. However, I presume I'll recover. Do you get spells like that—when you feel almost too lazy to wash yourself—and don't give a darn about anything—don't read—don't go to shows—don't think—just live from day to day in a daze—well I have that sort of a spell on and I hope to goodness I get over it soon.

Haven't heard from you in quite some time. Is everything OK? How is your boy friend? If he comes to California in the fall, give him my address and I'll boost your stock to him. Has he called you up since you met him at your Cousin's house? I'm very much interested to know of any developments.

With love to all, I remain, As ever,
Valeria

P.S. I thought I could come East in the fall, but now Mr. Goldwyn doesn't intend going away until November and I really don't care about coming to the East in the winter, so I don't know when I'll come home.

JULY 14, 1925
Dear Irma:

I received your letter—thanks so much for the four leaf clover. Not that I don't need all the luck I can get—but I hope the finder will share equally with all the luck that comes my way—at least enough so that you can soon come West again to see me as from the way things look now, I doubt that I can get away. I'd just love to see you again, because I really have so much to say that I can't write to you about.

It's awfully warm today, but there's no humidity—in fact, there is quite a breeze blowing—therefore Mr. Goldwyn has gone to the beach for the afternoon and I have nothing to do.

We are shooting two wedding scenes today—Lois Moran and Douglas Fairbanks Jr. in the Stella Dallas picture and Vilma Banky* and Ronald Colman in The Dark Angel. Both brides have beautiful lace metal dresses and gorgeous veils—the brides' maids look pretty too and the sets of both pictures are very artistic. I am going to watch them take these scenes because I know they will be interesting.

Vilma Banky and I are very friendly—she calls me 'darling' and in her broken English, it sounds rather funny. No doubt she doesn't know the real meaning of it, but she hears others use it so she uses it too. Mr. Goldwyn has put her into my custody, more or less. That is when it comes to telling her little personal things which he can't do, he has me do it. For instance, she doesn't dance very well so he said to me "You tell Miss Banky that you go to such and such a dancing school and you find it very good and tell her you think she could like it very much. It is fine recreation and it is good for you. You make arrangements for her and call up some good dancing studio and see that she goes." So then I have to tell this to Miss Banky, but not mention Mr. Goldwyn said it.

Another thing, she is troubled a little by stomach trouble and consequently her breath is a little offensive. Therefore Mr. Goldwyn asked me to get some kind of salts and tell her I took them and suggest that she take them too; that they would help her get acclimated

*Vilma Banky wore her bridal costume again when she wed the actor Rod La Rocque de la Rour (his real name) in June 1927. After trying to fan a romance between Banky and Colman for the publicity benefit, Goldwyn paid for the wedding, made it a huge Hollywood production, and even gave the bride away.

to this country and would make her feel good. It's rather funny my doing little things like this, but I really don't mind because after all, it's better than a job where you don't come in contract with anybody at all.

As for Ronald Colman, my admiration for him is gone. I don't know why, but he just doesn't thrill me at all anymore. In fact, I find him rather dull and uninteresting. I still, however, retain my admiration for Henry King and I think King knows at least that I exist, because whenever I go on the set watching him direct, I notice that when he sees me he calls out "tutto pronto" instead of "Ready, camera" and then I notice that he'll mention other Italian phrases such as "adagio", "bastanza", etc. As for Fitzmaurice, he still kids me whenever I go on his set, so I don't go anymore because it really embarrasses me. Fitzmaurice and Florence Vidor will eventually marry now that Florence has gotten her divorce. King Vidor who is Florence Vidor's ex-husband has been going about with Eleanor Boardman—in fact, according to rumors, she has been living with King Vidor for some time. No doubt they will eventually marry, unless King switches and hitches his affections to another star.*

Alice Joyce, who is playing the part of Mrs. Morrison, is beautiful—she is so dignified. Her little daughter—about 8—comes to the studio every day and Miss Joyce seems very fond of her. Owen Moore who was her former husband [and before that, the former husband of Mary Pickford] called me up a few days ago to find out if the little girl was here. It seems that he is the father and is anxious to

---

*Florence and King Vidor had married in 1915, separated two years later, and divorced in 1924. King and Eleanor Boardman married in 1926 but Florence Vidor, who had once dated Sam Goldwyn, did not marry Fitzmaurice. Instead she wed the violinist Jascha Heifetz in 1928.

see her, but Miss Joyce won't let him. Miss Joyce's present husband is James Regan—he's quite distinguished looking and comes every night to take her home.

Well, my boss is now connected with the United Artists, but until we know the outcome of Stella Dallas, I can't expect to get more money. However, if Stella succeeds, I certainly hope to come in for more money. I presume Mr. Goldwyn is satisfied with my work because he hasn't been disagreeable as yet, and Mrs. Goldwyn keeps telling me rather flattering things about me. By the way, we just had an opening in our office today for a secretary to our publicity man. Salary is only $25.00 per week but it is a good chance to learn the business. I've called up every girl I know (which is not really very many) and as they all have better jobs I haven't succeeded in getting anyone yet. Since I've been at the studio, I could have gotten jobs for at least 4 girls. I suppose if there was any girl I knew out of a job, I wouldn't hear of any jobs—that always seems to be the way.

Now I am going to tell you an almost scandal about myself. One of Florence's boy friends has been taking me out at various times (his name is Harry Lentz and is a teacher) and I rather liked him. Since Florence went away, he's been around about twice and the second time he came, he proposed to me—but not marriage. He suggested getting an apartment for me and everything else that goes with it. Needless to say, I was astounded. I asked him whatever gave him enough courage to even think that I would listen to such a thing. Can you imagine it, he said, "You are so unsophisticated that you are refreshing. I wouldn't suggest such a thing to a girl whom I thought stepped out with men."

It is certainly beyond me where men get their nerve. Things

certainly seem turned around in this country. My unsophistication used to more or less protect me, but now since this quality seems to be at a premium, I am subject to insults in the same way as if I were a street girl with no morals at all. It certainly is strange. Well, I sent Harry away and I presume I won't hear from him again. I'm rather sorry, because as I said above, I rather liked him. I'm wondering if he proposed the same thing to Florence. I wouldn't dare let her know, because at one time she was considering marrying him, but for some reason or other, their friendship broke off and she didn't hear from him for about 2 months. I suppose he's an irresponsible sort of man and I shouldn't have liked him in the first place, but in spite of his faults, he was really likable. I suppose this is just one more experience which will help me to understand humanity. I'm making quite a study of it and have lots of material to work on at present.

I'm surprised to hear that your affair has not developed. Listen here, don't you talk about your youth going quickly and all that sort of thing. Why, you have everything in your favor—you're tall, stately, distinguished looking and even good looking and have what most young girls haven't got and that's poise—and yet you bemoan your fate. Why, if you wanted to, you could have what I call a hell of a good time. Life is short and happiness is doing the things you want to do—providing the things you want to do are normal and right—and I am sure any pleasures you desire would be the right kind. Also a person has a right to be a little selfish—don't think too much of the other fellow. This sounds like a paradox but very often one's unselfishness is selfish. You know, when I was home, I was continuously doing things, not because I wanted to do them, but because I was afraid of hurting someone or due to some idea of sense of duty. In view of this, I wasn't living my own life. Now, I do just what I want to do and I'm much happier and I believe I'm really fitting myself to do the thing I desire most—and that is to write. I don't know if I'll ever amount to anything, but what difference does it make whether I do or not—I don't want to write because I think I'll make a fortune or a name for myself. I want to write because that is the thing which will give me the most pleasure. I didn't intend to moralize, but I had an idea in mind and it just popped out and after it was done, I realized it sounded like a sermon.

I haven't been to any shows or movies for ever so long. I've done a little reading—"The Flower of the Drama" by Stark Young—these are just dramatic criticisms, but very interesting. There is an article about Duse which I enjoyed very much and also some Theater Guild plays. I've read a book dealing almost entirely with sex—quite risqué—called "Replenishing Jessica" by Max Rodenheim. It's rather shocking, but conveys a new point of view—therefore interesting.

There isn't much more to tell you so I must end this letter, which I am afraid will be somewhat boring in view of its length. Nancy and I are still together and we will go into a smaller bungalow the first of August. I'll let you have my new number as soon as I know it.

Give my love to all your folks and when you find time, write to me again soon.

Yours for self expression, Valeria

AUGUST 21, 1925
Dear Irma,

I've delayed writing to you because I have really been very busy. We are all working at feverish heat in the studio. Our companies have been working even on Sunday and as for King, he works almost every other night—all night—sleeps a few hours—then goes on again. He looks a wreck and so does everyone else in the company. "Stella Dallas" will be finished in about 2 weeks and Mr. Goldwyn expects to give it a special theater in New York—have a regular premiere and for this reason I have just made out a contract with Louis Gottschalk who is writing special music for the picture. I suppose you saw the story about Belle Bennett. When it came out in Los Angeles, she came in to see me and she cried so—it was pitiful to see her. I don't know how the story ever got out—she thinks Goldwyn published it in order to get publicity for the picture.

Fitzmaurice has finished "The Dark Angel" and I attended the preview of the picture down in Venice last week. I wish you could have seen all the stars that turned out to see it—Norma and Constance Talmadge, Mr. Schenck, Marion Davies, Mr. Hearst, Rudolph Valentino, Elinor Glyn, Mary Philbin and lots of others. The picture is very good—you must see it when it comes around.

Now for a choice bit of scandal. You remember I told you that Valentino had picked Vilma as his leading lady. Well it seems they are going around together quite a bit. Last night Valentino took Vilma to the preview. Everybody was astonished at this. After the preview, the party I was with and myself walked around the piers and didn't go home right away. Quite some time later we went home and we rode behind Valentino's car—and Vilma was with him. This morning, the whole studio was talking about it and the papers carried a big story regarding it too. Mr. Goldwyn asked me to get Vilma to come over to see him—I located her in Valentino's bungalow! She came over and I kidded her a bit before she went in. I heard Goldwyn tell her that she must not do anything that will in any way ruin her reputation, etc. etc. When she came out, she gave me a wicked wink and said in her charming broken English, "Before, Marion Davies unt everyone else zay look at me unt zay nozzing," (with this she raised her head, lifted her shoulders and turned her nose up indicating that they all more or less snubbed her). "Last night with Valentino, Marion Davies zay 'Hello Vilma' so I will go wid Valentino—eh?"

It didn't take her long to catch on and with Valentino of all men who was supposed to be so attached to his wife. However, I can hardly blame him because she is really very pretty, whereas Natasha is anything but good looking.

Fitzmaurice felt quite elated over the success of his picture—he called me "Carina" in Italian and every time he sees me he either talks to me in Italian or kids me about something or other. Mr. King also talks to me in Italian quite a bit so that I'm rather glad that I know something about it otherwise I'd never even get a tumble from either of them I suppose. At least if Mr. Goldwyn doesn't know or isn't aware of my existence, his directors are friendly and in a way that makes up for Goldwyn's lack of friendliness. By the way, Mr. Goldwyn is getting awful—I was on the verge of quitting a few days ago. He expects just a little too much of me. I'm supposed to know what he's thinking about without his telling me. However, as my clairvoyant powers are nil, I just can't do it.

I read with interest regarding your brother's new enterprise. I see no reason why it shouldn't be successful and I sincerely hope that "Minute Maid" will bring you the things you want.

I keep receiving the papers for which I am exceedingly grateful. Mr. Mordant Hall, the critic of the Times, spent his stay in California at our studio. We gave him a room and he was our guest. He was very interesting and got quite a kick out of working in the studio.

Regards to all, Valeria

Dear Irma,

I'm writing to you again this evening because I'm so unhappy. All the girls have gone to Arrowhead over the Holidays and I'm home alone because as I told you yesterday I had to go into work today and Mr. Goldwyn asked me to be at the studio tomorrow (Labor Day) at nine. However, I am not so unhappy about being alone, but because I was disappointed in the picture [*Stella Dallas*]. I don't know what to say—it looks like a flop to me. When the picture was over, Mr. Goldwyn and Miss Marion asked *my* opinion regarding it. I told them what I thought, so Mr. Goldwyn wants me to come in with him tomorrow and we are going through the picture again and see what can be done about it. When I came out of the projection room, Mr. King was standing outside. He looked at me so tragically and asked me how I liked it. I really didn't have the courage to tell him the truth— he must know without me telling him—so I said that it really touched me and that with good titling he had made a marvelous picture. So far, we've spent $350,000.00 on the picture and if it's not a success, it means that Mr. Goldwyn will lose about $100,000.00

I was in the projection room from 10 until 2 and had to make notes in the dark. After seeing the picture and then having to eat my Sunday dinner alone, I just felt so blue that I cried until I came to my senses and realized how foolish I was. I bucked up and feel much better now although I can't take away from my mind the sight of Mr. King. I had so much confidence in him and then to see the mess he made of Stella Dallas—it really hurts me. Miss Marion feels awful about it too and can't understand how some of the things in it happened. For instance in some scenes, Laurel is shown with straight hair and short and in others it's long and wavy and then again in some places it looks bobbed and there are any number of technical faults about which I can't go into detail.

I know you are interested in "Stella Dallas" and I'll keep you posted as to how it eventually comes out. I'm of course presuming that all this "shop talk" doesn't bore you. You see, I'm so interested in it that I naturally feel that everyone else should be interested too.

Remember me to all your folks and let me hear from you soon.

Valeria

....

Henry King remembered the first in-house screening a bit differently. He had worked until the early-morning hours editing the film and went back to his bungalow at the Ambassador for a few hours' sleep before Goldwyn called him to come to the studio on Saturday morning to watch it with him. King begged off because of exhaustion but met him after the screening.

"I saw the projection door open and Sam came out. I went over to Sam but he didn't say a word. He was just staring into space. He looked at me and sort of quivered. 'Henry,' he said, 'You've ruined me.' Honestly, my heart sank. 'What do you mean, I've ruined you?'"

Sam pointed to Valeria still standing back by the projection room. "'She can't speak. I can't speak. It's Great. It's Marvelous. It just ruined me!' I had never seen him so emotional."

So in Henry King's memory, Valeria's response was silence over the emotional wallop she had just received from seeing the movie, not her fear for its future.

....

SEPTEMBER 12, 1925

Dear Irma,

I just received your letter and as usual I was happy to hear from you. I had a very depressing week, but feel much better now mentally.

About Vilma Banky and Valentino. I don't want you to have a wrong impression of her. She is really very sweet and didn't wreck Valentino's home. You see it's like this (I got the dope straight from Valentino's publicity man). Mrs. Valentino is very ambitious and for the last year has been devoting all her time to business and Rudy contends that he wants a woman who is at home when he gets home and who is a companion to him. Now Natasha was certainly not a home woman and therefore Rudy can hardly be blamed for losing interest in her. Furthermore, on account of her tactics, she pretty nearly ruined Rudy's career and if it hadn't been for the fact that Mr. Schenck signed him up (Mr. Schenck took the precaution of having a special clause inserted in the contract to the effect that Mrs. Valentino could have absolutely nothing to say or do with any of his productions) why Valentino would be up against it now.* Valentino

---

*In less than five years Rudolph Valentino had shot to stardom, and his tango in *Four Horsemen of the Apocalypse* alone grossed almost $4 million. Yet in the process, Rudy went through several

is a very quiet sort of chap. Very dignified, polite and ultra-refined. He doesn't mingle with the usual Hollywood crowd and doesn't go in for wild parties at all. Vilma is the same type—therefore they enjoy each other's company a great deal. They both love the outdoors— good books—art—music—so personally I don't see why she should not go with him. You know of course the marriage bond is quite flexible amongst theatrical people and judging from the conduct of others—I think their affair is not at all vulgar. In fact, I know their relations are not at all intimate, they are just friends.

I really feel sorry for the movie actors and actresses out here. They are continuously hounded by reporters and if a movie actor is seen twice with the same woman, there is sure to be a long report about it in the papers. Ronald Colman told me that he hasn't been seen in public with a woman in a year. He is living the life of a hermit just in order to avoid damaging publicity and this is true of a lot of others. Of course that is how they act here, but you know occasionally they go out on the town—to New York or Europe and then I suppose it's a different story.

Percy Marmont is on the lot making a picture (his dressing room is just a few doors down from my office) and he is very charming. A real Englishman dontcha know. He has such a good face, but I don't know yet whether or not his looks reflect his character. Dorothy MacKail is also on the lot and John Barrymore is here too. I just got

---

studios, two marriages, bigamy charges, hits, and flops. The lavish independent films his second wife, Natasha Rambova (née Winnifred Shaughnessy in Salt Lake City, Utah), encouraged him to make tarnished his career and left him broke. When Joe Schenck signed Rudy, he insisted on banning Natasha from the set. Some saw Schenck as Rudy's savior; others, like Gloria Swanson, believed Joe took advantage of Rudy's weakened financial situation to insist on total creative control over Rudy's projects.

a glimpse of John Barrymore so I really can't tell you how he looks. Corrine Griffith and Colleen Moore are both on the lot making pictures and of course Valentino is here too, so at the present time there are quite a galaxy of stars around. We've finished shooting both pictures so that we have no companies working at the present time. However, we are starting to cast for our next picture which will be "Partners Again" (that's a Potash and Perlmutter picture) but we won't have any big stars in it because it is a Jewish comedy. However, when Fitzmaurice starts his picture, which will be some time in November, we'll have quite a company because it's going to be a super-special.

Regarding Stella Dallas, we are negotiating for a theatre in New York (we might get the Apollo theatre) and give it a run of about 10 weeks. Personally, I don't think the picture will stand up. I was really disappointed in it and unless the titles will make it more interesting, it struck me as being rather dull. However, Frances Marion thinks it's good and there is no doubt that her judgment ought to be more reliable than mine.

Louis Gottschalk just finished a special musical score for it which I understand is very good and has written a song about Laurel—that's the daughter of Stella. The picture is going to be previewed at San Bernardino and after the preview I will be able to give you more information about it.

I'm sorry that Florence (that's the girl that lived with me in Los Angeles last winter) didn't get to see you when she was in New York. She has just arrived in Los Angeles and told me that she saw Mary Tarello, but on account of limited time, she was unable to see you. By the way, she met a Russian assistant director on the boat and she brought him around to the house and we've struck up quite a friendship. He is working on the lot next to ours and from the way he talks, I anticipate having quite a gay time this winter. His crowd stages masquerade parties—studio balls and other affairs and he is going to have the three of us get in on them. I've also met another fellow, Bob Nicholson, who seems to be quite interested in me. I have been out twice with him and have been to a party at his home. However, I'm afraid I shall have to quit seeing him because I have an idea he is still married. He told me that he was divorced from his wife, but I'm not so sure of this and there's no way I can check up on him. That's about all I have to tell you about my intimate affairs.

Things are getting a bit dull—I suppose being in so much excitement at the studio, unless there's something on every night, I get bored. I sure will have to get busy soon and do something and settle down a bit. I'm continuously on the go and I am afraid if I don't calm down a bit, I'll be a nervous wreck. I really am ashamed of myself—I do little or no reading—I don't go to concerts and I haven't seen a legitimate show in months. When I get home, I'm either exhausted and don't want to go out or if I do go out, it's to a party. It seems that the men out here don't like to go to shows—they either want to go to someone's house or go riding. I don't know whether they do this from choice or because of financial reasons, but whatever the reason may be I'm getting a bit tired of it. I'm supposed to call Bob up tonight and go out to dinner with him, but I'm not going so that I presume from now on he will be out of my life. Outside of Mr. Charsky (the assistant director that I met through Florence) there are no other men in my life.

Now that you have my history, I will proceed with something

else. Mr. Goldwyn is coming on to New York at the end of October and if I can possibly make it, I'm coming too. I've already told Mrs. Goldwyn that I think Mr. Goldwyn ought to take me along, because I'll be able to help him when he's in New York and at the same time look after my own affairs. She thought it was a great idea so that the first opportunity I have, I'm going to ask him about it. If I don't succeed in getting in on the N.Y. trip, I'm going to ask for two weeks' vacation and I'm going to a place called Valley Ranch in New Mexico. I heard of the place through Mr. Selwyn's son (that's the Selwyn who has the New York theatre) and it impressed me so that I'm going there for two weeks. Mr. Selwyn (we called him Sonny) was here with Mr. Goldwyn for about three weeks and Sonny spent all his time here at the studio. He's only about 15 and we had lots of fun with him.

Miss Franklin and I are on the outs. She was awfully good to me, but I didn't like the idea of her spending money on me and I didn't quite like her attitude towards things in general so that I have never called her up and quite naturally, she hasn't called me.

I'm still receiving the papers—I wonder if I can ever compensate you for your kindness in sending them to me so regularly.

Give my love to all,

As ever,
Valeria

P.S. I'm sending a fan photo of Vilma and Ronald—our stars—I know you'll boost them. Vilma gives a marvelous performance in The Dark Angel—don't fail to see her (I'm fast learning the technique of publicity)

SEPTEMBER 20, 1925

Dear Irma,

Well, it's Sunday again and I'm at the studio. I was here until 8 last night and before I left, Mr. King asked me if I wouldn't be so kind as to come in again today and naturally, I couldn't refuse him. Miss Marion, Mr. King and a special title writer and myself are retitling Stella Dallas so that it will be ready to be previewed tomorrow night at Pasadena. We had one preview of it in San Bernardino last week. I don't know whether I told you about it—if I haven't, I wanted to say it went over "big". However, this doesn't mean much because most of the people of San Bernardino are ranchers and their opinions counts for naught.

Several weeks before the San Bernardino preview, King, Goldwyn, and Marion had all met to go over the film. King remembered Sam saying, "I think *Stella Dallas* is great, but I don't know how to sell it. I've always had girls on horseback, in bathing suits.'" *Stella Dallas* was to be his first United Artists release, and he wanted to sell it with a bang. The group decided they would add a scene where the Ed Munn character has a drunken nightmare complete with delirium tremens and animals appearing in and out of his consciousness. "That's just what we need," Goldwyn said, "something Big."

King, like Valeria, remembered the San Bernardino preview as a success, yet the delirium scene did not have the effect they were going for. The scene was spectacular, but it so altered the mood of the film that the theater manager himself came up to Goldwyn afterward and said, "This is a great picture if you cut out that damn nightmare." Sam agreed and told King, "I was wrong. Take every foot of it out."

....

We are giving a special midnight showing of "The Dark Angel" Friday night. It's an invitation affair and only the movie colony is invited. However, I have an invitation so I'm going and am having a new outfit of clothes: black satin dress trimmed with ecru embroidery, wide flare skirt, big puffed sleeves, a bolero with sleeves attached to the bolero so that for business I wear the sleeves and for other occasions I leave off the bolero and I have a sleeveless dinner dress. I'm getting a black coat trimmed in wide bands of squirrel—the fur extends all the way down the front—the back of the coat is flared at the bottom and I have a new black velvet hat trimmed in gold and silver leather. My descriptions I suppose are awful, but the things are real nice. They are being made by a very chic dressmaker (used to be a Vogue designer in New York). She has a lovely shop and carries only very exclusive things. I met her through Belle Bennett, as she makes clothes for her. These clothes are costing me quite a bit, but I've worked pretty hard so to my mind I think I'm entitled to them.

Mr. Goldwyn is coming to New York in October because regardless of whether we have a good picture or not, he is going to open "Stella Dallas" in a Broadway theatre. We are negotiating for a ten week run in the Central, Apollo or Embassy theatres.[*] I expect

*Goldwyn booked *Stella Dallas* into the Apollo Theatre on 42nd Street in New York.

to get a two week vacation when he goes and as this will be too short a time to warrant my coming all the way to New York, I'm going to spend it at Valley Ranch, New Mexico.

I just received a letter from one of the girls in Langner's office and I was surprised to learn that Mr. Langner has married Armina Marshall. She is the girl I was introduced to by him and whom I visited just before I left N.Y. I was supposed to go to her people's ranch down in Imperial Valley. At the time, Mr. Langner introduced me to her, I hadn't the remotest idea she would be the next Mrs. Langner. Mr. Langner wrote me some time ago, but I didn't answer his letter until after he had already left for Europe so that I suppose my letter is still in the office. However, he is expected back this month and I suppose I will hear from him soon.

Florence has come back from the East and we are going to live together again. We've just rented another apartment which is nearer to the studio and is larger than any we've had before. We are paying $65. a month, exclusive of gas, electric and phone, but at that it only comes to about $25.00 for each of us. We have a very large sitting room with a wall bed, and one end or corner of the room is a little dining room suite. Our bedroom is quite large and we have a nice double bed in it so that it will be quite comfortable for the three of us. I've just counted up the places I have lived in since I've come to California 1) Buckingham apartments 2) Y.W.C.A. 3) Sierra Vista Apts., 4) Daily Hotel 5) 1520 3/5 Reid St. 6) 1520 1/5 Reid St. and now No. 7 is 4168 Oakwood Avenue. I can't complain about the monotony of always being in the same place.

I have no boy friends now—lost them all. My last was Bob Nicholson. I think I told you in my last letter about him and about having a dinner engagement with him which I intended to break.

Well, I didn't break it because he came around and made such a fuss that I had to go. After dinner, we went to a show and after that, I would rather tell you than write. Anyway it's been another experience and I presume it's the last I'll see of Bob—in fact I don't think he will want to see me. I'm just so disgusted with men in general that I'm devoting my entire time and attention to work now—of course the problem still presents itself at the studio—all the men in our production unit are married—but that doesn't prevent them from attempting to make love to you at any opportunity possible. However, I'm so busy that they rarely get a chance to be funny with me. Occasionally, when I have to go on one of the stages or some other department someone will try to hug and kiss me, but I manage to wriggle out of their reach most of the time. I'm not quite used to such affection and demonstration that when it does occur, I blush furiously and then of course this incites much laughter and then men get a great kick out of seeing me blush. Of course I realize that it's all done in fun and sometimes I think I'm just a little too narrow. But you know how it is when one has been brought up in a conventional atmosphere and under the strictest of moral codes, it's hard to be otherwise but prim.

You want to know what some of the movie people get—well, beginning in our own organization, Colman gets $2000 a week, Belle Bennett $500 a week, Frances Marion gets $10,000 for each continuity she writes, Fitzmaurice gets $50,000 for each picture he directs and 50% of the profits of each picture. King gets $75,000 for each picture and 25% of the profits.[*] As for the other big stars,

---

[*]Goldwyn had his two directors under profit-participation deals, in part to limit production costs; he said, "You spend a dollar of my money, you are spending a dollar of your own money."

I know they all get immense salaries, but I'm not sure how much. Gloria Swanson gets around $15,000 a week, Thomas Meighan about $10,000 a week.

The weather here is glorious, but awfully dry. We haven't had a bit of rain since about the 10th of June. One day is just like the other, hence you can never open a conversation with "Isn't this awful weather we're having?" which you must admit is quite a drawback in making new friends, especially with the opposite sex. When I meet a new fellow, all I can say is "Aren't the stars bright tonight!" or some other such dumb remark—and that ends it. You just have to talk about other things or appear stupid.

How is Ida's baby getting along? She must be quite cute now. Is your sister Mary feeling better? Why doesn't she take a trip to the coast—I'm sure she would enjoy it. I suppose Isabel is doing the Charleston—I want to try to learn it myself although I think it's quite a crazy dance. Nevertheless, one must keep up—you can't let these flappers put things over you.

Give my love to all and write me soon again.

As ever,
Valeria

[This letter, although dated, starts without a salutation, so its first page might be missing.]

SEPTEMBER 26, 1925

This is certainly a neat way of Charlie and Marion extricating themselves from an unpleasant or rather unfortunate affair. Charlie really was going to marry Marion and was very much in love with her—they were to be married about the same time that he was involved in the Lita Grey affair and was forced to marry Lita.

Do you remember when Thomas Ince suddenly died on a yacht party? Well, Marion Davies, Hearst, Charlie Chaplin and a number of others were on that party and according to the wild rumors around the lots, it is said that Hearst became very much incensed over the attention Charlie was paying Marion—after a few drinks, they got quarrelling about it and Hearst either shot at or threw something at Charlie. Charlie ducked and Ince got the blow and died a few hours after.

I don't know how true this tale is—but I've heard it from a number of people and they all seem to believe it. I can't really say that I believe it because I know how ready people are to talk and I usually give anyone the benefit of the doubt until I'm positive. Anyway, I have passed this on to you as I thought you might be interested in knowing what rumors go around.

Saw the special showing of "The Dark Angel" last night—it is a beautiful picture and went over great. I had my new outfit on and it felt good to get new clothes on again. I think the picture is going to open at the Strand on October 11th. I know you will enjoy it.

Am going to a beach party tonight—we are going to build a big fire on the beach and have supper there. This seems to be quite a popular diversion for the "younger set" in Hollywood. I've never been to one before so I'm looking forward to having a good time.

Sunday morning Nancy and I are going on a hike with the Sierra Hiking Club. We leave at six in the morning and there will be about

100 in the party and we will ride in busses to the mountains and then hike.

Love to all,

As ever,
Valeria

P.S. We are looking for a very dramatic and romantic story (not costume) for Fitzmaurice and suitable for Colman and Banky. Story must have strong heart interest and of course story must not be censorable. Can you suggest a book that you have read or a play you may have seen? It doesn't make any difference how long ago you saw the play or read the book. —VB

....

Thomas Ince was a pioneer Hollywood producer and director; he had created his own film studio and back lot called Inceville, made literally hundreds of movies, including the groundbreaking *Civilization,* and moved on to be a powerful third, along with Mack Sennett and D. W. Griffith, of Triangle Productions. Ince was a hard worker and a hard drinker, with a reputation for claiming credit for his directors' work. He had amassed a small fortune while the stars and workers he hired, notably William S. Hart, were kept at surprisingly low salaries. By 1924 Ince was no longer the major player he had been, but he was still famous for creating stars, and William Randolph Hearst, obsessed with having Marion Davies at the top of the popularity charts, was meeting with Ince about a possible production deal.

There are very few sure facts around the death of Thomas Ince in November 1924, including the names of the other guests on board Hearst's 220-foot yacht, the *Oneida,* when it left the harbor for a long weekend at sea. Everyone agrees that, besides Ince and Hearst, those present included Marion Davies and Hearst's studio manager, Dr. Daniel Carson Goodman; most accounts add Charlie Chaplin, the novelist Elinor Glyn, the actress Seena Owen, and Marion's sisters, Ethel and Reine. The actress Margaret Livingstone, who was reportedly Ince's mistress, is often mentioned, but Marion Davies specifically denied it, claiming she "didn't even know her." One biographer, in trying to replicate the event, concluded that "if everyone rumored to have been in the stateroom had been there, it would have been more crowded than the one in *A Night at the Opera.*"

Undisputed is that Ince was in the party on the *Oneida* and then left the boat early on the morning of November 17 at San Diego. Dr. Goodman accompanied Ince, who was suffering either from acute indigestion or from a bullet wound. They were on the train to Los Angeles when Ince's condition worsened, and they got off and went to the Del Mar Hotel. Goodman then called a doctor and Ince's wife, Nell. She in turn called Ince's personal physician who, according to her, had been treating Ince for ulcers and "symptoms of angina pectoris" for some time. Ince's wife and physician then went together to the Del Mar, where they arranged for an ambulance to meet them at the station in Los Angeles. The four of them boarded the train north, but instead of going to the hospital upon their arrival, Ince was taken to his Benedict Canyon home, where he died two days later at the age of forty-four.

Speculation abounded that Ince had actually died after being shot (in either the head or the stomach) by Hearst, who had mistaken him for Chaplin, who was having an affair with Marion Davies. Yet the newspaper accounts at the time were relatively restrained, and few even mentioned Hearst's name. Only one edition of the *Los Angeles Times* and an article in the *New York Daily News* intimated that Ince had been shot.

Although most reports had Ince dying in the early hours of Wednesday November 19 of "angina pectoria" [sic] after an acute attack of indigestion, the *New York Times* had him suffering an attack on a train to San Diego the previous Monday and didn't even have him near the yacht. *Variety* claimed "he died suddenly at his home" and went so far as to proclaim that "his demise at so early an age is believed to have indicated the tremendous inward and nervous energy Ince must have expended in racing to the position of wealth and influence he occupied."

The *Los Angeles Times*, owned by the Chandler and Otis families, was the rival publication to Hearst's *Examiner* and would therefore have had an assumed interest in bringing down or at least denting Hearst's influence. Adela Rogers St. Johns, who had been a Hearst reporter and columnist before turning to writing scenarios and fan magazine articles, loved a good rumor and asked her friends at the *Times* what they found out. She claimed that the *Times'* reporter A. M. Rochlen told her "he covered every moment from the instant Tom Ince left the yacht, interviewed the water taxi driver who took him ashore, and the train crew and from there on through doctors, nurses, undertakers, police and coroners. He then had to go back and tell Mr. Chandler there was nothing to it [the shooting story]."

Ince's remains were cremated within two days of his death, but his wife said they had agreed upon cremation and there was no question in her mind that he died of a "fatal heart attack." Ince had a history of digestive and stomach problems exacerbated by his drinking and, though hardly medical confirmation, Jack Gilbert and Leatrice Joy's daughter, Leatrice Gilbert Fountain, always remembered her mother telling her Ince had the loudest and most virulent burps of anyone she had ever known — or heard.

No inquest was held to investigate Ince's death, and neither the Los Angeles district attorney nor the county coroner touched the case. San Diego district attorney Chester C. Kempley looked into it and found that "there is every reason to believe that the death of Ince was due to natural causes [and] there is no reason why an investigation should be made." Kempley interviewed only the doctor and nurse who had taken care of Ince at the Del Mar Hotel, and both said that Ince had told them he had drunk "considerable liquor aboard the yacht *Oneida*." Even when reporting these details, the *New York Times* left the name of the owner of the yacht out of the article. The clear implication from the San Diego officials was that if, during Prohibition, inherently illegal liquor had been on board, it would have been obtained in Los Angeles and was therefore out of their jurisdiction.

This story served to shift the rumors from murder to the illegal possession of liquor, but even then Hearst's name rarely figured in any newspaper report. And while the stories would stay alive through the Hollywood rumor mill, none of the guests ever talked for the record to confirm anything but a heart attack.

It is interesting that Charlie Chaplin chose the next weekend to finally marry his pregnant, seventeen-year-old girlfriend, Lita Grey, and Hearst returned to New York and did not attend Ince's funeral. Hearst stayed away from California for a month and chilled, albeit very briefly, his relationship with Davies. Another story told over the years was that Hearst took care of Ince's wife and children financially, but Ince left an estate of more than $4 million. And even if the dozen or so friends who were on board could all be silenced, what about the crew of at least thirty people who were also on the yacht?

Still, the Ince "murder mystery" rumors have stayed alive and were even the source material for an embarrassingly poor film, *The Cat's Meow*. Another ripple effect of the story that has made its way into the category of "common knowledge" is the idea that Louella Parsons had a job for life with Hearst because of the Ince affair. Rumor had it she had been a witness on the boat and her silence guaranteed her employment. However, Parsons's columns that winter, including the day before the yacht left the harbor, were datelined New York, and her first recorded trip to California was not until the following summer.

The light that Valeria's letter shed on the story, besides her recitation of the rumors roiling through the studios at the time, is the following handwritten notation, dated September 30, 1951, on the side of her letter:

> Lucy told me when in Venice that Louella Parsons has her job with Hearst because she was a witness at the time this took place. Maybe it's just another rumor.

Her comment helps date the time this story grew to credence, twenty-five years after the incident (it is the only postdated note Valeria wrote on any of the letters and presumably reflects the time she received the letters back from Irma). Parsons's name was not mentioned in any of the original stories at the time of Ince's death, nor was she the power she would become. The early 1950s is also when Louella was at the top of her game as a Hollywood columnist, pitched in feverish battle for "scoops" with Hedda Hopper. Back in 1924, Hedda Hopper was still an actress; she did not pick up her pen as a columnist until the late 1930s.

....

OCTOBER 1925

Dear Irma,

Thanks for your card—it was sweet of you to remember my birthday. It seemed so good to know that somebody remembered me.

Things are very slow now that Mr. Goldwyn is in New York—in

fact after we finish "Partners Again," we are not going to do another picture until next Spring. In the meantime, I believe we are going to loan Mr. Fitzmaurice to Mr. Schenck to direct the next Valentino picture. You know since "The Dark Angel" has met with such tremendous success, Mr. Fitzmaurice is considered quite a big man—and naturally he takes his importance very much to heart—acts sort of swaggering, but nevertheless, his attitudes towards his subordinates hasn't changed a bit. He comes to the studio for about an hour every day and of course he always talks to me in Italian. Yesterday he said "Come sta la mia piccolina" in very sweet tones and of course I replied in Italian "O bene" then I said something about his being a "grandesimo homo" and he bowed all over the place saying "Mille grazias" to me. It certainly is strange, no matter how big a man is, he likes just a little flattery. Of course, women do too, only one woman seldom flatters another sincerely and when a man flatters a woman, the wise woman takes the flattery with a grain of salt.

I am still receiving the newspapers from you and I hope it's not too much trouble for you to send them.

I don't know whether I've written to you before about it, but I've sent you a book—it's futile for me to attempt to repay you for your many kindnesses, but I can't think of sending you anything better than a book that I like. I know you will like it too. Try to read Willa Cather's "My Antonia". I can truthfully say that nothing thrilled me more than "My Antonia".

Give my love to all the folks.

Valeria

OCT. 27, 1925

Dear Irma:

I'm just dropping you a hurried line to tell you that one of Nancy's boy friends is in New York and I gave him your office address so that he could call you up. He's an awfully nice, quiet chap—I like him very much. His name is James Kent and I'll appreciate your trying to make him feel at home in New York. He wrote sometime ago that he was quite lonesome and I therefore gave him your address and told him to call you up.

I was at the Mission Inn in Riverside on Sunday. It's just as romantic as ever. I'm enclosing a petal from one of the roses which our publicity man brings me every morning from his garden. Isn't it a pretty shade? The roses he brings me are beautiful—he's a bachelor, but I don't stand a chance with him considering that he hob-nobs with all the movie stars. Anyhow, I'm content to get roses from him. We have lots of fun at the studio, especially now that S.G. is away. My dignity has gone to the wind and I feel as carefree as a child of ten. I guess I act like one too. I put on all the jewelry and head gears and whatnot and we pretend we are acting something tragic. Our publicity man is inclined to be stout and between Marie (King's secretary) and myself we sure do make him go some. We Charleston all over the place and all in all I guess an outsider would think we had gone nutty. You know how it is when one has to be very dignified and reserved most of the time and then you have an opportunity to let go—why you just let go. There's no harm in our play and we may as well play while we can.

When I started this note I only intended it to be a short one, but it's turning out to be a letter.

By the way, I just found out we live in the Wilshire district. Last night on my way home from dinner, Ruth and I walked down our street and were remarking how beautiful it was—the sky was a deep blue and the stars were so twinkly—the street is a broad one and lined on both sides with huge palm trees. The houses are all set back with lovely lawns in front (everything is quite a new green now since the rain we've had) and the pale moon shining through the palms threw weird shadows on the lawns. It looked so enchanting, Ruth and I just stopped and drank in the beauty.

Ruth is Schenck's secretary and we are quite chummy—she is very emotional and since I'm quite a bit emotional myself, we get along pretty well. She was so glad she was in California and away from the cold and snow of Minneapolis and I was glad to be here and away from the cold that I know will come in New York. Ruth is the girl who has the car and as she lives near me, she picks me up every morning and takes me to the studio. I sure do think of the many years I commuted from Jersey to New York and I'm rather grateful that I don't have to do it anymore. Now I have no carfare at all to pay and I get home in about 15 minutes. However, there is one thing I do miss and that is eating at home. I eat out most of the time and while I go to a pretty little tea room where I get a nice dinner for 75 cents, it gets rather tiresome eating out all the time and I'm just too lazy to cook. I can't eat with Flo because she gets home from school about 4 and gets her meals prepared and eats by 6 o'clock and of course I wouldn't ask her to cook for me. Nancy works in Los Angeles and of course she eats downtown before she comes home. Ruth and I sometimes eat together when we happen to get off at the same time. I'd give anything almost to have my usual family dinners and be around a table with the same people every night. I can't very well arrange with a family to eat with them because I get off all hours at night so that I suppose I must reconcile myself to eating out. One can't have everything. You must sacrifice something for freedom.

I'm going to try to get "The Perennial Bachelor." Just now I'm reading "The Glorious Apollo". It's a biography in novel form of Lord Byron, the poet. Quite interesting.

Love, V

NOVEMBER 3, 1925

Dear Irma,

I just received your letter and I was shocked to hear about Ida's marital difficulties. I was under the impression that she was very happily married and quite surprised over your letter. I'm glad to know that she is taking the whole situation courageously and everything will in the end come out all right. She has her baby to look forward to and that ought to be a powerful incentive for her to 'carry on'—more so than for you and I—if we succeed, who benefits by our success?

So you expect to go to Florida for your vacation. What will this be, your winter vacation? I had an idea you had a vacation this summer. I hear there is a great boom going on down there and people are flocking to the state from all over. Nancy was quite anxious to go and was trying to get me to go with her—but somehow, I felt I ought to stick to my job and since I couldn't be persuaded to go, why Nancy decided to stay here too.

Ronald Colman got back today—just bought a Packard straight eight roadster—I was outside admiring it when he came along—he took ahold of both my hands and said how glad he was to see me again and told me about the good time he had in New York, etc. etc. I told him how all you girls liked him so much and he acted quite shy about hearing this. He is ideal—but I could never get excited over him—he is just a trifle too ideal to make me realize he is human. I like our fat little publicity man much more.

I haven't taken my vacation as yet, because we are in production and Mr. Lehr is so busy that I hate to ask for time off. There isn't much for me to do, but the little I do do is so confidential, that Mr. Lehr feels I must do it and no one else. Furthermore, Mrs. Goldwyn left me in charge of their home and servants and I have to attend to paying them and the household bills and anything else that comes up.

Sunday Flo and her boyfriend and another girl and her beau and I (I was beauless) went to the Museum of Art and as I was walking around, whom do I see but our publicity man! I was so excited—I started to walk over to him—when curses! The closing gong sounded and everybody flocked to the door and my man was lost to view. My spirit was crushed for a moment, but I rallied and although fate played me a dirty trick, perhaps it was for the best. We all then went to an Italian restaurant—stopped to inspect a new Catholic Church (one of the boys is an interior decorator and he wanted to see something in the church) and then we went to one of the girls' apartment. She called up a few fellows and a little party developed. There were some boys in the next apartment and they came over with two Hawaiians who had guitars and ukes so they played and we danced and a good time was had by all.

About 8 girls have gotten together and we play bridge one night each week and meet in each other's homes. Life is beginning to shape itself more like the life I led at home, so that I'm quite happy, I'm not tired of Los Angeles—of course we don't live right in town, we are nearer to Hollywood where it is quite country like and I just love our place.

Mr. Schenck's secretary, Roland West's secretary, Mr. Schenck's reader and myself have formed a class and we take French lessons on the lot twice a week during our lunch hour. Today was our first lesson and we all enjoyed it very much. Mr. Jomier is quite a dapper Frenchman. He is very well known in the colony and has given lessons to all the movie stars.

It seems to me you are going to do a lot of heavy reading this winter—if you get through "Thus Spake Zarathustra" you're a better man than I. There's a lot of good stuff in it, but as a whole it is rather incomprehensible. The book you mentioned has already been considered, but Fitz didn't like the story. As for "The Rat" I believe some film company has already bought the rights to this play.

Am anxiously awaiting a snapshot of you in your new clothes. You know you've never sent me anything of yourself.

Valentino is going to be in N.Y. for the opening of "The Eagle" and Mr. Schenck wired Goldwyn to have Vilma come to N.Y. and also make a personal appearance with Valentino. Mr. Goldwyn just wired us to explain to Mr. Schenck that in view of the relations between Mr. and Mrs. Valentino and the fact that Vilma is quite friendly with Valentino, it wouldn't be good policy to have Vilma in N.Y. when Valentino is there too and the Mrs. So Vilma is not going to N.Y. Mr. Goldwyn can't afford to have any scandal to arise around Vilma as that would be sure to kill her popularity.

Saw "What Price Glory" the other night which is very good. Lots of swearing in it—but it sounded good, strange to say. The picture "The Big Parade" opened at Grauman's Egyptian Theater and it's a tremendous success. Everybody is just raving about the picture.

When you see "Stella Dallas," I wish you'd let me know just what you think of it. Ethel Barrymore has just seen the picture and she's written the loveliest letter to Mr. Goldwyn. He sent a copy on to me and has also told me that everybody is talking about the picture in New York.

I dropped Franklin about 6 months ago—today I had a few hours off to do some shopping and was walking along Hollywood Boulevard and if I don't run into her! That is where I met her after we had dropped acquaintance the first time when I went north with you and it seemed strange to run into her again in the same place. I promised to call her up, but I don't think I will—from the looks of her face, I don't think her disposition has improved any.

Jimmy Dugan is back again as assistant director to King. He seems very nice now—I suppose being out of work several months sobered him up a bit and his attitude towards me has changed completely. He treats me now like a co-worker and doesn't proposition me every time I attempt to talk with him.

I could go on telling you lots of little things that occur every day, but I'm afraid I'll be getting like a gossipy old woman, so I had better quit before that happens. Give my love to all and write me a nice long letter soon.

Valeria

NOVEMBER 27, 1925

Dear Irma,

I received your various notices on "Stella Dallas" and I was so thrilled to read them. I'm so happy that the picture went over big and all that I'm waiting for now is to hear your reaction to the picture. Mr. Goldwyn arrived yesterday (Thanksgiving Day) and as I wasn't to the studio, I didn't see him. He's not coming in today because he has a sore throat, but I've talked to Mrs. Goldwyn over the telephone and she told me all about the opening night—how wonderful it was and after hearing about it, I certainly am sorry that I didn't come to New York even if I couldn't stay longer than 4 or 5 days. Now I'm hoping that the picture will make so much money that Mr. and Mrs. Goldwyn will decide to go to Europe for the summer and I will then subtly suggest that they ought to have me go along—I'd be willing to pay my own way—accept a salary of say $10 a week and do his letters and wires while abroad which wouldn't take up more than 4 or 5 hours of my time and the rest of the time I could have for my own. If this could be arranged, I'd certainly consider myself lucky because I figure on $10 a week, I could live quite well in Europe and outside of my traveling expenses, I'd be covered. Wouldn't it be nice if you come too? Say, we'd paint Paris red, wouldn't we?

I'm going to a Hollywood party tonight. I don't think it will be a very wild affair, but I'll give the details that led to same. Nancy, Flo and I went golfing one sunny Sunday morning and we met two (gentlemen?) on the links. They took the 3 of us riding all afternoon—stopped at Pasadena at some beautiful estate where one of the fellow's cousins lived and procured a bottle of cognac. They bought a lot of food and we all came to our apartment, ate, had a cocktail, played baccarat and a fine time was had by all. Since then one of the men has taken a fancy to Nancy and has taken her out a number of times. The other fellow (His name is Jones and he's about 65) calls up and occasionally takes Flo to work in the morning, and I'm left in the cold. However, I'm not worried about that because

I wouldn't want either one of them. Nancy and Flo are inclined to be gold diggers and try to get as much as they can out of every man whereas I would rather stay home than go out with a man just for the sake of going out. The fellow that is taking Nancy out has a home in Hollywood and his people are in Texas for the winter and he's asked us to go to a party that he's giving. He said he would have a fellow there for me and I am wondering now just what he will be like. I'll let you know how it turns out.

Michael Arlen is in Hollywood and while I haven't seen him I've spoken to him over the phone a number of times because Fitzmaurice is very friendly with him.* Arlen gave a party last week and when asked to give a speech, this is what he said: "Well, I hope you all have a damn good time because this party is costing me a helluvalot of money." That was all he said. This is what Fitz told me when I had to get Arlen on the phone: "You better call him a few hours before the engagement and remind him of it, because he's crazy as a bat and full of hop and Hollywood."

Nov. 28th—cont.

Mrs. Goldwyn just brought me 5 beautiful silk handkerchiefs from New York. I was so pleased to know that she gave me a thought when she was so busy with other things. Mr. Goldwyn is still sick and today he sent down his town car and chauffeur to take me up to his home where I have to take some wires. They have a gorgeous place—they are renting it from Mrs. Compson (Betty Compson's mother).

---

*Michael Arlen was a prolific and popular British writer and the author of *The Green Hat*, turned into the film *A Woman of Affairs* for Greta Garbo.

I feel rather all in today after the party last night. It was not at all wild—in fact there was nothing at all to drink. The fellow they had for me was very nice—he plays the piano beautifully and is a professional singer and while he isn't what I would term good looking—when he sings, you just forget what he looks like. We danced and sang and talked until quite late and for some reason or other I couldn't sleep the few hours I had left to sleep in and consequently I'm all in today. That old fool Bob Nicholson called me up at the studio again last night and still has the supreme audacity to invite me to a party. There's no way of insulting him—he just keeps calling me up and asks to take me out.

I'm sending you a picture of Ronald Colman taken the other day. This is taken right in front of our offices on the lot. This is a rustic arbor with rose vines and the trees are acacias. During our lunch hour, this is where I sit with some of the girls and when my boss is out, I sit out there and can just run in when I hear my phone ring. The different stars' dressing rooms are all along here and across the street are the stages. All the pictures I get of Ronnie I send on to you so I hope if I ever come back to New York, perhaps you will let me have a picture in case I should not be able to get one for myself for some reason or other. I think this is a good picture of him, don't you?

I had rather a quiet Thanksgiving. Flo was invited out to her boy friend's home for dinner and Nancy went to the Clark Home with 3 other girls for dinner. I had lots of things to do, so I stayed home alone and met Nancy and the 3 girls downtown Los Angeles in the afternoon when we went to see Mantell in "As You Like It." After that we went through the art gallery in the Biltmore Hotel, went to the Greenwich Village of Los Angeles to look up an artist friend of Nancy's who unfortunately was not in his studio and then I had my Thanksgiving dinner in quite a fashionable restaurant. Nancy accompanied me, but she didn't have another dinner. Then we took the bus home and thus ended our day of Thanks. I had been rather depressed for a few days, but when I thought out my case, I felt I had something to be thankful for. When I consider that about a year ago I arrived in Los Angeles sick, friendless and jobless, I think I have something to be thankful for when a year later, I have health, friends and a good job, so I immediately cheered up and am in the best of spirits again. I suppose you had a good time considering the size of your family and that you all are more or less happy and prosperous.

Remember me to all your folks and looking forward to a letter from you very soon, I am as always,

Valeria

DECEMBER 8, 1925

Dear Irma,

Your letter of November 23rd was received and I'm not sure whether I acknowledged it or not. Your cousin Lena has not called on me as yet. I do hope she does because I'm dying for the sight of someone who knows you.

Mr. Kent has left New York and is now in Florida. I'm sorry he didn't call on you—you would have liked him I know. I hope you'll find me pictures of your mother taken on her birthday.

Sam is back and I'm terribly busy. By the way Sam is very friendly now with Hearst and Marion Davies. At the opening of

"Stella Dallas," Mr. Goldwyn asked Hearst to join their party and Hearst sent a letter to Sam enclosing an original telegram from President Coolidge asking Hearst to dine with him. I wonder what Coolidge is conferring with Hearst about?*

Colman comes around daily and looks as wonderful as ever. He sure is a knockout. Doesn't bother with women at all. Another man that's good looking is Lloyd Hughes.

Jimmie Dugan's four year old son died yesterday. You know about Jimmie having attempted to be nice to me—however on this last picture he's been a perfect gentleman. It was quite sad—Jimmie had told me only the day before that the boy was taken to the hospital because he had a 106 degree fever, but the doctors couldn't localize the trouble. The next day the boy died.

We also had a serious accident in our picture. In one scene, an aeroplane runs along side an auto—the plane ran into the car—the camera man's skull was fractured and the other occupants were hurt too, but not seriously.

Vilma Banky came in today with a large photo of herself autographed to me. I thought it was awfully sweet of her to give it to me. You know I would never ask an actor for a photo. Would you like a personally autographed photo of Ronald? I might be able to get one for you. Tomorrow night I am going out with a real artist— Bohemian and everything—he has a studio in the Latin quarter of Los Angeles. The three of us girls are going together. Nancy's friend

*W. R. Hearst, in addition to being a film producer, was one of the richest and most important publishers in the country. Film bosses were becoming such high-powered executives that by 1928 Louis B. Mayer was the highest-paid man in America. Mayer was such a fervent supporter of Herbert Hoover that he would be the first guest to spend the night in the White House after Hoover's inauguration.

is an Italian artist, Flo's man is a writer and mine is an artist too. I haven't seen him yet, but I am told he is quite interesting. However, the Italian artist told me he has a mistress and she is Madam Zucca who has one of the most Bohemian of cafes in this town. I suppose therefore we won't be going to Madam Zucca's—otherwise there might be a dead wop.

There's been another artist around the studio who has been trying to get me to go to his studio—he's a married man. The only reason he thought I was a bit gay was because I told him one day that while I had an artist temperament I could not very well display it—being a secretary I have to be very business like—so he said "Well, if you'll come to my studio, you may be as temperamental as you like—and I'm sure we'll have a wonderful time—however. I will have to exact something from you and that is I'll paint a portrait of you, providing you will pose in the nude." Right then, I knew I made a mistake someplace and I became very business like immediately. It is a funny world out here—everyone seems to be romantic and seeking adventures—even I.

Today has been a regular July day—in fact it has been wonderful right along. I certainly would be the happiest girl in the world if I had some of my best friends out here too. I do long to see everybody again. However, I wouldn't want to live in the East anymore. The year I have been in California has been one of my happiest. I don't know when I shall have time to write you again. You will excuse me won't you because I really am very busy. Sam is going back to N.Y. at the end of this month so after he is gone I'll have time again to write you.

With love to all,
I am as ever, Valeria

DECEMBER 29, 1925

Dear Irma:

I just received your letter and I am hastening to reply to it because it so happens my boss is out of the office this afternoon and I have an hour to spare. Thanks for your good wishes. I also received the picture you sent me and it was mighty fine of you to think of me.

All your good wishes have come true—I had the most happy Christmas I've ever had, that is so far as material things are concerned. Naturally at heart, I still miss my mother and all my friends and I can never be really happy until there is someone who can in a measure fill this gap.

Everybody at the studio was wonderful to me—Ronald Colman gave me a lovely underarm bag, Frances Marion gave me a gorgeous French beaded pocketbook, Mrs. Goldwyn gave me a pair of black satin mules trimmed in green ostrich feathers, Mr. Fitzmaurice gave me a huge box of candy, Mr. Lehr gave me a gold cigarette holder (I smoke occasionally now—but it's not a habit as yet) and I got things from about 5 or 6 other men at the studio. The office gave me a week's salary.

The day before Christmas we had a little party at the studio in the afternoon—of course everybody had been drinking but me—I had to remain sober because I had to send about 75 telegrams out for Mr. Goldwyn and flowers to wives of his business friends. Mr. Goldwyn left about 3 in the afternoon and then the fun began. I had about 5 assistant directors in my office, our production manager, Jack Pickford, a few minor actors and then Ronald dropped in. As I said before, I was the only sober one in the lot, however they were not disgustingly drunk—just funny. Ronald is making a picture with Norma Talmadge—"Kiki". Did you see it in New York? If you did, you know the type of picture it is.[*]

Well, Ronald came off the Kiki set and he was still in his make up and feeling pretty good. It was the first time I had ever seen him like that—he's always so quiet and reserved and almost unapproachable. He put a cap on me and wound a muffler around my neck and then I put on my black satin mules with the ostrich feathers and Ronald and I were playing "Kiki". I'd sit down in my get up and write a wire and I'd just get through when he'd pull me up and go through some scene he had just gone through with Norma. You can imagine how I got those wires out—since they were only Christmas greetings, if there were any slip ups, it won't be of any consequence. Then Ronald was trying to do the Charleston and couldn't—he looked awfully funny. Finally we tried it together and it was worse. Well, to make it short, we had quite a hilarious time. I finally had to send Ronald home because he was giving a party at the Ambassador and I wanted him to be able to at least receive his guests. I went home about 7 and then Nancy and I and a fellow we know went out driving. We drove until about 2 in the morning and then dropped in at Coffee Dans (it's too bad you didn't see this café while you were in Los Angeles—it is quite picturesque) for breakfast.

Christmas day I slept until 12 and then went with a married couple and Nancy to the Paris Inn for Christmas dinner where we

*Ronald Colman was under contract at $2,000 a week, and without another film ready for him, Goldwyn "loaned out" his star to United Artists at $6,000 a week to make *Kiki*. It was common practice at the time for the studio to pocket the difference in salary and that is exactly what Sam did.

spent the evening.* This is a very Bohemian place (that's where our artists friends hang out but they weren't there that night) and the owner is a Turinese so we became acquainted and he was lovely to me. Introduced me to a lot of people and it so happens that he is the brother of the fellow I had met through Nancy's artist friend. By the way, this fellow I met wanted me to go up north with him on his ranch—he was in Los Angeles for a week visiting his brother and he took me out every night and from what I can gather he really wants to marry me. Isn't that rich? When the man who owns the Paris Inn found out I was the girl that went around with his brother, why he just put himself out to see that we had a good time. This fellow that wants to marry me is supposed to be quite wealthy—has an immense ranch—but he's rather unpolished and I couldn't think of marriage to him. He's all right to go out with occasionally, but that is all.

These last three weeks I seem to have gotten in with a regular "Greenwich Village" set of people and needless to say I have been having a wonderful time. Perhaps you wouldn't approve of some of these people—you know how funny they dress—and how unconventional they are—but dog gone it—they are interesting and you talk about things that ordinary run of men do not find interesting. Jones, who is a writer, has given me a book to read called "Fathers and Sons" by Turgenev—it's quite interesting. Jones and I have long talks on books and Muschi (Nancy's artist friend) and I talk about art. Another woman of the crowd has a Russian ballet studio and another man Froelich is a noted sculptor. In view of all these people, I'm again interested in the arts and since you go to lectures

*Although a Los Angeles city ordinance forbade dancing after midnight, the Paris Inn was one of the few restaurant-clubs where dancing went on all night.

106

in the museum, I know you would enjoy these people, even though you have to more or less overlook their moral characters. Most of these people are not married—just live together and they seem really happy. Muschi absolutely does not believe in marriage and he's trying his best to get Nancy, but Nancy of course doesn't believe in such things so she just kids him and keeps him on the string. He intends to go to Paris this spring and has suggested that I go too (if Nancy won't go). Of course I admire Muschi very much—he's very intelligent and a very fine man and since he likes Nancy so much, I know he wouldn't attempt to make love to me, so that I'm almost persuaded to go in case he does. Do you think my reputation would be marred in any way if I traveled with a man who is almost old enough to be my father (he's cross eyed too). He's awfully interesting and I know I'd meet a lot of interesting people if I went with him. What do you think of it?

Well, I have to quit and I guess it's about time I do. I don't suppose all this chatter about people and places that you know nothing of interests you much, but if I don't tell you these things, there is nothing else I can tell you. My life has been so full of excitement this last month that I just can't begin to really tell you everything. I suppose next month I'll be bored to tears. That's how things usually go.

With love to all and apologies for this rambling letter, I am

As Ever,
Valeria

P.S. Did you get the box of figs I sent to your home in West New York? I ordered these for you before you told me about your contemplated change of address. My other artist friend at the studio who wanted me to pose in the nude sent me a Christmas greeting of a girl in a very artistic nude pose. It's really quite good and I'm going to send it to you just so that you get an idea of it.

Dear Irma:

As Mr. Goldwyn is in New York again, I'm not so busy and today Mr. Lehr has gone for the day—hence this letter.

Irma, the weather is simply gorgeous—so far the rains haven't yet come and every day is just lovely and warm. It's so nice to be able to sit by an open window and see the green grass and trees while you work. Where we live we have a little lawn and plants and I noticed this morning one of the rose bushes in bloom—one of the roses being wide open and the rest buds. The calla lilies are also in bloom—it just doesn't seem possible that it's mid-winter. Last winter it was colder because we had quite a bit of damp weather and around Christmas we had a little frost in the morning and at night. However, this winter I don't think the thermometer has been below 60 and during the day it's always around 75.

Just now I'm typing the story we bought "Beauty and the Beast" by Kathleen Morris. As the action takes place in Italy (Sicilian mountains) I'm wondering if Fitzmaurice will take any scenes over there. I wish he would and take me along—that certainly would be the realization of my hopes and dreams.

I'm still going around with that Bohemian crowd I told you about. Last Saturday night one of the sculptors gave a studio party and I was invited. He is a very noted sculptor and has busts of many of the prominent people in the world. At the party I met an Italian sculptor who did the statue in Pershing Square in Los Angeles and quite a number of other things. He's an old man about 65 but very charming—he speaks Italian beautifully and he is so poetic. We danced together and I really enjoyed the evening—more so than I had anticipated—you know what wild rumors you hear of these studio affairs, but they are not quite as bad as they are painted.

I also met two fellows who are decorators for all the Biltmore hotels. Both were of Italian parentage and although American born, they speak Italian quite well. One of them was particularly nice and before the evening was over, we were quite chummy. The next day, around 9 in the morning, my new friend called me up and wanted to know if we couldn't get together and spend the day with them. He suggested we go up to his studio and have our Sunday dinner there. It sounded good to me so he sent a taxi for us and we went. I noticed a few things around his place which seemed to indicate that a woman must be around and I said something to that effect and he said, "Oh that belongs to the woman who comes in to do our cleaning." Well, we had a nice dinner and we played and danced and sang and then he took me home around 8 o'clock. On the way home, he admitted he was married and that his wife was away on a concert tour for about 2 months and wouldn't I let him come to see me occasionally. Of course I wasn't surprised because I rather suspected it, however I really couldn't be angry with him because he was very nice and there was really no harm in spending the day together like we did. However, I told him I would rather he didn't see me again because if there is anything I dislike more it is to be entangled in some scandal of that sort and while there may be nothing wrong in his seeing me occasionally, you never know what may develop.

I am going to another studio party this Friday with the same crowd and I am wondering if he will be there—in a way I hope he will be—because I enjoy his company and if I see him with a crowd around I think it will be perfectly safe.

Nancy and Flo are both keeping steady company and I imagine it won't be long before they are married. They both stepped around with a lot of fellows—none however ever proposed marriage with the exception of those and I think they are both grabbing at the chance even though both the fellows in question are not quite what they expected to marry.

How are your folks? Is Ida still with you or has she gone back to her husband? What about Isabelle? You never speak of her—I presume she is getting along O.K. and also your mother.

I thought you might be interested to know that Mr. Hearst and Marion Davies bought toys for about 1000 children this Christmas. They both went shopping together and they were just like school kids. Miss Davies is also building a new asylum building for the children—costing about $50,000 and she bought about 25 acres of ground for it. One of the fellows at the studio who is an architect is building it and has told me of some mighty fine things they are both doing and that is not published. He tells me Miss Davies is very nice and quite big hearted and goes out of her way to help people. Of course he's all for her because she gives him a lot of jobs and pays him well. However, I understand from others too that she is good hearted. I think you will notice that where people slip a cog or so, insofar as morality is concerned, they usually make up for it in some other quality. In my experience, I find that nearly all the people who are really big or have done big things cannot be examined too closely when it comes to a question of morals.

Write to me soon and give my love to all.

As ever,
Valeria

P.S. I'm enclosing a Christmas card Lew Cody sent Mr. Goldwyn which I thought you might like to have because it's a good picture of Lew. I'm also enclosing one of the many dumb letters Mr. Goldwyn receives but which of course he never sees even though they are marked "personal and private".

FEB. 2, 1926
Dear Irma,

I haven't heard from you in quite some time but as I have been receiving the usual papers from you I know you haven't forgotten me—no doubt you are quite busy. Since my boss has left, things have let up a considerable bit and I find myself with little or nothing to do at the studio.

Ronald was in today and dictated a letter to me. He had just come off the Kiki set and was dressed in a dinner coat—striped trousers—spats, etc. He is really fascinating—more so than on the screen. As he was dictating, he pulled out of his pocket a pink crepe chemise (you know in the Kiki play, Kiki puts in his pockets bits of underwear instead of handkerchiefs in order to arouse his interest in her) and he flourished it about rather unconsciously. No doubt he forgot he was off the set. I looked at him and smiled and he realized what he was doing, blushed and put the chemise back in his pocket.

I'm sending a few samples of the inane fan mail he receives. He gets an average of 400 to 500 such letters every week and I thought you might be interested in some samples.

You know of course that Fitz is going to direct Valentino in "The Son of the Sheik" and Vilma is going to play opposite him.

When King gets back from New York, I'm going to ask him if he'll take me on as his secretary and script girl. Of course, I don't know that he'll have me, but I may as well try for the job.

The only dirt on the lot now is that Pola Negri today drove to Albuquerque to meet Valentino. She has an awful crush on him. When Joe Schenck heard about it, he wanted his press agent to drive after her and prevent the meeting because Schenck is afraid there'll be some adverse criticism and scandal, but it couldn't be done so I suppose it will get out in the papers.

Huntley Gordon is still on the lot and very distinguished looking. He surely has it all over these young sheiks.

I've been having some awfully good times lately and through Muschi I'm meeting ever so many distinguished people. Sunday afternoon Muschi took me to a sort of soiree at a studio and met 6 or 7 singers of the San Carlo Opera Company. (They are now in Los Angeles for 3 weeks). They all sang bits from the operas. Pedretti the sculptor was there. He showed me the formal invitation he received to exhibit his works at the Pennsylvania Academy of Fine Arts which is quite an honor. I also met the editor of the Italian paper in Los Angeles. We had real champagne and other sparkling wines and delicious imported delicacies. I also met a most interesting young fellow who has promised to write to me. It was a case of love at first sight—of course I don't know what it will be at second, because who knows I may never see him again, even though he promised faithfully to write to me and see me again. We stayed at the party until 9 and then went to Jones' studio where we met some more interesting people.

I've just bought myself an orchid taffeta evening dress trimmed with silver lace and silver kid slippers. You see one of the boys I know (he's a tenor and gives vocal lessons—his name is Howard Clark) invited me to an affair and I had to have the outfit for this occasion. Howard also composes and he asked me to write a poem and he would write the music to it. This is what led to his making this request: When he took me home, on my doorstep, I felt he was going to ask me to kiss him. I didn't want to so I immediately became poetical. I gazed up at the sky—the moon was full—and all the stars that could possibly crowd into the sky were twinkling and the palm trees looked so beautiful swaying in the soft breeze—well, I just made up a lot of foolish nonsense to distract his mind. I guess I succeeded because he said, "Why don't you write some love lyrics and I'll write the music to them." So we immediately forgot everything else, but just what we were going to do and he went away contented much to my delight because I really don't care for him and I just couldn't love him. He calls me up nearly every night to find out if I've written anything and I'm just about all out of excuses to avoid seeing him. I hate to tell him point blank that I don't want to see him. It sure is a funny world—someone that you don't want, wants you and someone you want, doesn't want you. Tis ever thus in this queer world of ours.

Our Nancy got married Saturday and is away on her honeymoon. We've gotten another girl to come in with us—she's a school teacher and seems to be very nice.

Tomorrow night I'm going to the Paris Inn for dinner and dance with a friend of Dr. Hansen's (That's Flo's boyfriend) and expect to have a good time.

How is everything with you? I suppose you are doing ever so many things and not flitting your time away like I do. You know, I just can't be domesticated. I have no housework to do nor washing and ironing so that the least I could do is to see that my clothes are in proper shape, but it never fails but that before I can go to work in the morning I have a button or a hook to sew or a hole in my stocking or some other fool thing and I cannot for the life of me think of doing what some of these lectures are about.

I could go on ad infinitum about things that would no doubt be boring to you so that the better part of my what used to be good judgment now counsels me to desist and as I always obey that inner voice, I shall end my letter without further ado.

Give my love to all your folks and write often.

As ever,
Valeria

FEBRUARY, 1926

Dear Irma,

It seemed like years that I had not heard from you so that when I received your letter I felt quite normal again. I'm sorry that you are not feeling well and I do hope that you are better by now.

Isabelle's letter certainly came as a surprise and I was glad to hear from her. I sent her a picture of Ben Lyon, which I hope will please her.

Have you read about the scandal in Tia Juana? It looks as if the place is now doomed and in a way it's a good thing because there were really disgraceful goings on. Outside of the time you and I were down there together, I have not been there since—although of course I've had a number of invitations.

Sometime in March we are going to move over on the Pickford-Fairbanks lot. All the United Artists will be on one lot—the Talmadges, Valentino, Mary and Doug, Charlie and ourselves—this will be a permanent studio and I think it will be quite nice. It's a little further out than we are now, but Mr. Schenck's secretary Ruth and I may get a place together near the studio. My plans to become a script girl to either Fitz or King are dashed—they are both employing men for the job because they have decided it's too strenuous work for a girl. In view of this, if nothing else turns up by next June, I'm going to give up my job with Goldwyn, coming East and then on to Europe and I expect to take about six months vacation. After that I shall settle down to a real comfortable life of bachelorhood. I'm going to have one more glorious year and then become a dignified woman of undecided age and live on my memories. How does this plan strike you? Of course I'm not positive I'll carry it out—I always have a sneaking feeling something is going to turn up. I guess I've got an adventurous turn of mind—anyway I imagine all sorts of things and I suppose nothing will happen though unless I make them happen. You know of course that nothing happens if you just sit around and wait for things to happen—you just have to go out and start something. Someday I suppose I'll get myself into trouble by starting something I can't finish but why worry about that now?

Nothing much has happened within the last two weeks—things have been rather quiet. I got two Valentines at the studio but I don't know who sent them (they were mailed from Los Angeles) and they were mighty nice. I wish I knew who thought they loved me so much as was mentioned on the valentines. I saw the play "Desire under the Elms" with a friend of the family—an old man about 55, bald headed. He's a research chemist for the General Petroleum Company and so intellectual. Can you imagine it—Los Angeles has stopped the play (the night after we saw it) because the language is obscene! Last night we went to see Leatrice Joy in person in a play called "The Candle." The Potboilers put the play on (it's an organization corresponding to the Provincetown Players and similar small theatres in New York).

We are starting work on Barbara Worth and it's going to be a marvelous picture. I suppose you heard that we paid $125,000 just for the story rights.* Frances Marion will get $10,000 for adapting the story, King will get $75,000 for directing it, assistant director gets $500 weekly, art director $400 weekly, technical director $300 weekly, Ronald Colman $1750 weekly, Banky $1,000 weekly and then all the minor assistants and actors, cost of costumes and building sets and then you can imagine about how much the picture will eventually cost. Of course you mustn't forget my $40 per—it makes me sick when I look at our pay roll and then look at my salary. I suppose though that I ought not to complain because there are others who don't get as much (that's what my mother always used to tell me when I was dissatisfied). However, I can't compare my lot with those who are more unfortunate than myself—can you?

Have you seen our new picture at the Strand? I personally don't think it's so good and it really wasn't Mr. King's fault that it wasn't.

* The Winning of Barbara Worth was a best-selling novel by Harold Bell Wright, so Goldwyn rationalized the price tag: if 3 million copies of the book had been sold, he assumed he was "buying an audience of 10 million people."

He didn't want to do the picture, but Mr. Goldwyn insisted and the result was the mediocre comedy.

By the way our mutual friend Marion Davies is stepping around again with Charlie Chaplin (I saw them at a Charleston contest the other night).

Haven't read anything lately—just some of Shelley's poetry. I have really lost most of my ambition. I hope that when I decide to become ambitious again I will be able to and get out of this lazy existence that I am indulging in.

With love to all and looking forward to seeing you next June, I am as ever

Your friend, Valeria

Dear Irma,

It's some time since I've written to you and I have so much to tell you that I don't know where to start, and if I do tell you everything, I'm afraid you will grow weary reading of my personal affairs.

There isn't much going on at the studio. Mr. Goldwyn is still in New York. Henry King is back and he is making trips down to Imperial Valley and environs hunting locations for Barbara Worth. Fitz is over on the Pickford-Fairbanks lot where he is making "The Son of the Sheik" with Valentino and Banky and of course I don't get to see him at all anymore.

No doubt you have read about the Negri-Valentino affair. I used to admire Valentino quite a bit, but I certainly don't admire his choice. Did I ever tell you what Hergesheimer told me about Pola? (By the way, read Hergesheimer's article covering his trip to Hollywood in the Saturday Evening Post—it goes quite into detail about stars, etc) You know he and I were very chummy and we used to talk by the hours about everything—however, mostly love, since he's quite an authority on the subject.* In the course of conversation he told me about Pola having a suite up at Del Monte where she entertained Chaplin privately in her apartment and believe they lived for awhile together there. Then, in Hergesheimer's words, "after her affair with Chaplin cooled off and Rod La Rocque was bewitched, if she didn't have the audacity to bring Rod to the very same apartment—in fact in the very same bed—where she had just previously had Chaplin. That, in my judgment, was unpardonable—the least she could have done was to have Rod in a different suite of rooms. However, that is Pola for you—brazen. If I had been Rod I would have left her then and there—but poor fool was only a toy in her hands and let himself be juggled about as she wished and utterly helpless."

This may sound crude to you, but you know authors, and in fact all artistic people, talk about things in such a simple, natural way that you cannot possibly take offence at the things they say. Hergesheimer occasionally would say things that would shock me a little. But I didn't dare let him know. He also told me about various types of women (and he seems to understand them pretty well) and all about Aileen Pringle and the Gish girls and ever so many other stars. By the way, here's another bit of dirt about Aileen Pringle. For quite a long time she and the art director at MGM lived together, then for business reasons the

*Joseph Hergesheimer was a popular novelist and short story writer. Goldwyn bought his novel *Cytherea, Goddess of Love* for a film (directed by George Fitzmaurice, starring Lewis Stone and Alma Rubens, adapted for the screen by Frances Marion, and filmed at United Studios). *Cytherea* was released in May 1924, more than six months before Valeria came to work for Goldwyn.

art director had to go to New York and this same art director came back from New York with a twenty year old girl whom he married in Hollywood and Aileen was the bride's maid—big hearted Aileen. She is noted for her generosity, especially in matters of this kind.

I have been having a wonderful time. My artist friend Muschi takes me to all the studios and I meet all kinds of people. The Bohemian colony in Los Angeles certainly has it all over Greenwich Village because here they are real artists and not fake ones like you find in the Village. I've just met a fellow through Muschi who is very much in love with me and although I've only seen him twice (met him last Wednesday) he's been sending me boxes of flowers and calling me up incessantly and tells Muschi different things to tell me. However, I'm indifferent to him because I know that he's been living with a girl for the last 8 or 9 months and has only recently left her. I told him this and said that I could never love a man who had led such a life. He was terribly sorry he had done it and explained the whys and wherefores of the situation and finally broke down and cried—ye gods! These artists are so child like—sometimes I want to laugh at them and then at times I really feel sorry because they are so sensitive.

His name is John and I don't know yet how the affair will develop—so far as I'm concerned, I'd rather it would be terminated immediately, but then on the other hand it's nice to have someone crazy about you and doing impulsive, unexpected things like sending flowers and notes.

Now I'm going to relate just how I came about to meet John. Wednesday night Muschi called up and asked me to come down to the Paris Inn and have dinner with him. When I got there, Muschi was there with John and Muschi asked me as a favor to him if I could play a little part to help out John. It seemed that the Spanish dancer and singer at the Paris Inn was so infatuated with John that she annoyed him with her attentions and they wanted me to pretend that I was John's sweetheart so that Carmelita would cease her attentions. Muschi begged me to do it just to help John out of this situation and as a favor to Muschi, I agreed. Well, my dear, Carmelita was furious and I wish you had seen the dirty looks she was giving me. She sang all her passionate love songs and danced all her wicked dances in front of our table and doing everything possible to taunt us and I pretended I was jealous and angry—it was great fun but rather dangerous for me. I danced with John and looked into his eyes saying sweet nothings and by the time the evening was over, I found much to my surprise that John was not pretending any longer and that he meant everything he said and he wanted me to be serious too. Poor Muschi just sat there and looked on and didn't know what to make of it.

They both took me home and John arranged that he, Muschi and Jones would come over the next night to our apartment and bring food and have a dinner there. I said O.K. so that the next night they were there promptly and John proposed and I refused and he got angry and left me, never, never to see me again. I said "farewell" and thought it was the end. Muschi also said "goodbye" because he said I was fickle and only pretended I liked him, etc. etc. So I felt I had lost them both, but I didn't worry although I did value Muschi's friendship.

The next night I came home and there were the flowers and a note from John and about a half hour later, Muschi calls up and takes me to Pedretti's studio for a party (that's the Pedretti I told you was invited to the Academy of Fine Arts in Pennsylvania and whose statue is in Pershing Square in L.A.) Last night John called me up and wanted to take me out, but I couldn't go because I gave Nancy a shower and had about a dozen girls at the house. So this is how matters stand now and I don't know where I'm at. Tonight Dr. Hansen is coming over with another doctor for me and we are going to some cafe, tomorrow night I'm going with Howard to a studio party (Douglas Fairbanks' art director's studio) and after that, I guess I'll be all in. By the way, I'm taking ballet dancing lessons. I've already taken two lessons and I just love it. The girls from whom I take lessons belong to the crowd and have their studio in South Pasadena.

Now I'll tell you something else I've done. I've cut my hair real boyish. I wear it slick back off my ears. Everybody seems to like it and it's so comfortable not having hair flying all over your face. Also I'm leaving my job in June, coming to New York for about three weeks and then I'm going to Paris for about three months then on to Italy. I've managed to save $1700 and I've decided to save about $300 more—spend $1,000 traveling—leave one thousand here and when I finally land up in Italy, I'll stay there about a year on my other $1,000 and endeavor if possible to do some writing. I'm all enthused about the plan. If I don't succeed in writing anything worthwhile in the year, I'll give it up, come back to America and of course I'll come back to California because I feel that I will be able to get another job at the studios at that time. How does that strike you? You know I'm going to be 28 and I may as well have a year in Italy at this time and do my traveling now before I lose all my pep and become a dried and cut old maid. Just one more year of fun and play and then I shall settle down. I think I've told you this before about settling down in another year so you must be convinced that I really mean it. I don't suppose you'll be able to take a little vacation with me to Italy, do you? I'm not spending money on clothes at all and look quite shabby, but I'd rather be a little shabby and be able to travel—wouldn't you?

I've gained about five pounds and all in one place (curses) in spite of the fact that I go swimming one night a week and practice my ballet dancing every night. I'm getting to look quite mature and rather dumpy so:

> Gather ye rosebuds while ye may
> For old time is still a-flying
> And that same flower that today is smiling
> Tomorrow will be dying.

Hence my decision to go abroad this June and jeopardize my prospects for a career at the studio. Do you approve?

Write me soon and looking forward to seeing you (I can hardly wait to see all you folks)

I am
as ever, Valeria

MARCH 31, 1926

Dear Irma,

This is just a line to let you know that we are settled at the DeMille Studios in Culver City.* Do you remember Culver City? The DeMille Studios is a big white colonial mansion. There is a negro in uniform standing outside the door and every morning when our

---

*United Studios on Melrose was sold to Paramount, and Goldwyn took up his friend Cecil B. DeMille's offer to move to his studio in Culver City. The mansion–office building, originally built by Thomas Ince and inspired by Mount Vernon, would later be made famous by David Selznick, who used the edifice at the beginning of his films, such as *Gone with the Wind* and *Rebecca*.

car pulls up in front of the studio, he runs down the steps, opens the door, runs up ahead of me and opens the door in the building and boughs [sic]. Never had such service in my life. I'm afraid I'm being thoroughly spoiled by everybody. Because I'm Mr. Goldwyn's secretary, I have any car at my disposal for nothing. I can get any kind of liquor delivered to the house and can you imagine it, the bank in Hollywood has informed me that even if I draw checks on my account when it's overdrawn, they will honor my checks anyway. It's rather hard for me to give up all these privileges because I may never get another job like it, but I'm quite decided about going to Europe.

Friday night "Stella Dallas" opens in Los Angeles and I'm quite busy calling up all the stars to come to the opening. I have two passes right in the star's section so that I'll have to start getting primped up for the affair.

Last night a publicity man I know gave me two passes to see Lionel Barrymore in "The Copperhead." I had seen this play in the movies quite some years ago, but it was revived on the legitimate stage in Los Angeles on account of Lionel being on the coast. While the play is interesting, Barrymore was awful in it. He's in a terrible condition due to dope.[*]

Do you remember Anton Grot, the art director who was at our studio when I first got my job and who tried to make love to me? I believe I told you about him and how glad I was when he left. Well, on arrival at the DeMille Studio, whom do I run into but my dear

---

[*]Barrymore had long suffered from arthritis. Another actor in *The Copperhead*, the very young Clark Gable, apparently went unnoticed by Valeria. Barrymore arranged for a screen test for Gable at MGM, and he was filmed against a South Seas backdrop with a hibiscus behind one ear. Unimpressed, the casting director said Gable's ears made him look like "a giant sugar bowl." Gable continued on the stage until he was "discovered" for films four years later.

friend Mr. Grot and to make matters worse, his room is right next to mine. He hasn't tried anything funny as yet. In fact, he's been most courteous and gentlemanly in his actions and perhaps our relations may be different here. I hope so anyway, because I rather like him and would like to be friends.

I'm not getting any new clothes this spring because I want to save all the money I can and I'll do most of my buying in Paris where clothes are much cheaper. I'll try to get along on what I have until I get to New York at the end of June and outside of buying just traveling clothes in New York, I'll do the rest of my shopping in Paris.

I had a half a day off last Friday and Nancy and another girl and I played golf at the Sunset Canyon Country Club. In driving up to the place I was thinking of you because we were on the same road that we were on when we went to Santa Barbara. All the peach orchards were in bloom—the beauty of the country just took my breath away and I was so thrilled. I certainly shall come back to California when I return from Europe. I don't think I shall ever be content to live in the East again—especially West New York. (Mr. Goldwyn's chauffeur just brought me a big bunch of violets and I'm enclosing one for you. They are so pretty and fragrant.)

Love to all – Valeria

I don't put any stock in what they say or promise until a thing is done! Yet I'm going to enjoy my stay in Italy very much if John comes too.

Carmelita has left the Paris Inn and has gone to San Diego—so I am safe in going out with John now and you need not worry about me.

Dear Irma,

I didn't mail my letter of March 31st so that this is a continuation of that letter.

Since writing you about John, I was out again the next night with him. We had a violent quarrel (I'll tell you more about it when I get back) and everything is over and I have no intention of seeing him again.

Friday night was the big night. "Stella Dallas" opened in Los Angeles. My party consisted of 6 and what do you suppose—you know how on opening nights crowds gather to see the stars enter and a little passage is roped off in front of the theatre so that the people stand on both sides and watch—well we entered and our publicity man who was standing beside the camera man told him to snap us because we were somebody or other. Practically all the stars turned out—what clothes! The ovation the picture got certainly thrilled me and I was just so happy that I was on the verge of tears. How I have prayed and worked for the success of that picture! Not for Mr. Goldwyn's sake, but for Mr. King's. Of course he was there and Belle Bennett, Lois Moran and all the other members of the cast excepting Ronald who is working on location in Yuma, Arizona. Some of the others there were Leatrice Joy, Charlie Chaplin, Mae Murray, Jack Gilbert, Eleanor Boardman, Vilma Banky, Jack Holt, Tony Moreno, Betty Bronson, Betty Compson, Lila Lee, James Kirkwood, Anita Steward, Von Stroheim, Lubitsch, King Vidor, Lillian Gish and others whom I can't recall. Rupert Hughes was master of ceremonies.

The picture is a tremendous success and yesterday the house was sold out completely.

Today is Easter and I'm quite alone. I've been out every night last week until 2 and 3 so that I'm just exhausted today and I've made no plans to go out. Flo is out with her Harry and Connie is out with her Dick and I'm here alone writing to you in my pajamas.

Connie and I had quite some bitter words the other night and if it wasn't for the fact that I shall be leaving soon, I don't think I'd want to continue living with her. She is very very nervous and high strung and acts so childish that she just gets on my nerves so that sometimes it requires all the self control I possess to keep me from doing or saying something real mean to her. It seems that her boy friend said some very nice things about me to her, which infuriated her so that she took it out on me. The next day Connie apologized and said that she was so jealous of Dick that she really didn't know what she was doing. At any rate she made such a scene (Dick was here at the time) that I was mortified and can't easily forget, especially since she had no cause for being jealous of me. After this, when Dick comes, I'm not even going into the sitting room to say "How do you do." I'll certainly keep out of their way. The strange part of it is that Dick doesn't interest me in the least and I have never even tried to be nice to him, therefore I just can't understand it all. Some women are such fools—and Connie is one of them.

I'm glad to hear that Mary—your sister—is feeling better and there's no doubt but that a stay on the coast would do her worlds of good.

Your Patricia must be a dear and I rather envy you all your relations. There are absolutely no prospects of my having nieces or nephews and I shall just grow old with no relations around me to take just a little interest in me. You know you can have lots of friends when you are young, but when one is old, it's not so easy and it's rather comforting to be an old aunt to a lot of young people. As for marriage, I could have married either John or Muschi, but I couldn't. They are artists and I know that it wouldn't last. They have both had such care free lives that they could never make good husbands. You know I was very much tempted to marry Muschi—he is so charming, talented, fine and interesting, but I worked out a chart as follows and decided the odds were against him.

GOOD:

1. Artistic soul
2. Appreciates music, books, art
3. Good natured and generous
4. Has many friends in the world of art
5. Doesn't drink to excess but likes his wine
6. Never has an unkind word about anyone
7. Understands humanity.

BAD:

1. Cross eyed
2. Outside of world of art and bohemians in general, he would be out of place
3. 45 years old and has believed in free love
4. Has always lived with some woman
5. Won't do anything but paint—therefore has little money
6. Admires all pretty women
7. Tolerant to a fault.

Under "Bad" point 5, I say he won't do anything but paint. Of course this is not really a thing to be counted against him, but if I'm married and he doesn't make any money and refused to do anything else, I'd be rather hard up so I've listed this as one of the bad features.

All in all, I guess I'll remain a bachelor girl and you and I will perhaps get together when we are old cronies.

In view of my break with John I suppose I won't get those letters of introduction and he won't be coming to Europe. No doubt I'll have a good time there without him. I sure do wish you could come too. The idea of traveling about alone in Europe doesn't quite appeal to me, but if I must, I'll have to do it because I won't forego my trip on this account.

This is what I think I'll do—First, I'll go to Italy, look up my father and establish a domicile. Then from there I'll start out on my trips. First around Italy and then I'll go to Paris for about 2 months and then spend the rest of my year in Italy quietly in some country town. Just now I'm so tired of going around and I'm just sick of Cafe life. Just as soon as I get into Madam Zumma's Inn or the Paris Inn, my spirits seem to drop—the gaiety seems so false. At first I was thrilled, but the sameness of everything is beginning to bore me. It's no use—this is not my mode of living and while I thought at first I had found the sort of life that appealed to me, I find I'm mistaken and that isn't what I want at all. I often wonder just what it is that I do want. Don't you feel that way too and wonder just what it is that will make you happy? Just now I feel that I shall be supremely happy when I arrive east and see you and all my other friends. I'm really looking forward to this event with a joy that is indescribable. To understand it you must be away from everybody you know.

My dear, it's already 10:00 A.M. and I've been writing for 2 hours and I had planned to go to church this morning. I just must quit.

Love to all,
Valeria

Thanks for your Easter Card. I'm glad you thought of me. I haven't sent you a card, but this letter is an Easter greeting. "Some greeting" you will say no doubt, but I mean well and really think of you often.

MAY 1, 1926

Dear Irma:

Things are getting pretty busy around the studio and now that I'm working on the Barbara Worth script, I find myself so wrapped up in the picture that I don't know how I'll be able to tear myself away until it is finished. If I do that, why I'll still be here in September and then perhaps I'll find myself so engrossed in Beauty and the Beast that I won't want to leave and I'll never get away at that rate, so I suppose I had better stick to my original plan. I haven't said anything yet to Mr. Goldwyn, but I hope to find an opportune time this week to tell him.

Our publicity man has just left—he's been offered a better job with the Hal Roach studios and I'm going to miss him terribly. We were such good friends. He used to listen so patiently to all my little troubles and love affairs. He is a confirmed bachelor and seemed to get an awful kick in hearing of my escapades with my bohemian artist friends. Our new art director is awfully nice—Carlo Borg (he did the sets for Douglas Fairbanks' "Black Pirate") and we have very interesting talks. I manage to drop in to see him for about 15 minutes every day—it does break up the day. The other art director—Anton Grot—is behaving himself, but I have to keep my distance. Every time I pass his studio he beckons for me to come in and have a chat, but I pass by and tell him I'm too busy to talk.

I wish you could see Rupert Julian (he directed Phantom of the

Opera and a number of other big pictures). He is such a dainty dresser. Wears pretty ties of delicate pink and sometimes a brilliantly colored silk scarf draped around his neck, etc. I don't think he is effeminate—not at all—but just dresses crazy. He is also quite affectionate, providing one gives him just a little bit of leeway. We are pretty good friends and he knows that I won't tolerate any funny business.

I have just met Adrian (he designed the costumes in "The Volga Boatman" as well as other DeMille pictures) and he is very effeminate—the men here kid him so—however he is very clever and his designs are very original in conception. I have met DeMille who attaches quite a bit of importance to himself—it's killing to see everybody bow to him and "Yes, Mr. DeMille" him.

Our new roommate has left us. It was too much for her to travel to Sawtelle every day and since she was a very nervous type of girl she decided it would be better if she lived nearer to her school, in so far as health was concerned. Personally, I'm glad she has gone because I had some very unpleasant experiences with her—experiences which I've never had in my life before. I wish you had been present at some of the sessions I had to go through when her boy friend was around. Well, things came to such a pass that when he called I used to sit in my bedroom until he was gone. Connie was terribly jealous and she seemed to think that her boy friend likes me. It's no use going into details about the matter, but when I see you, I'll tell you some of the crazy things she used to do. While I was embarrassed many times and was really furious at her, I never really quarreled with her—I'd just let her talk and I'd keep my mouth shut because I realized that she was really to be pitied and it was useless coming back at her. Flo and I are going to keep the apartment and not take anyone in with us because we will only be in it for two more months.

I haven't been going out very much during the last month. I'm still studying ballet dancing and have only been to two parties with Muschi. Saturday night Jones had a dinner party at his studio and I was invited with Muschi. Much to my embarrassment, my ex-boyfriend John was there. However, I didn't recognize him and treated him like a complete stranger. Most of the evening I stayed in the back sitting room with Muschi and two other men and we were talking on socialism and art and music, etc. One of the men had read all the German philosophers such as Kant, Hegel, Nietsche, as well as August Strindberg and Shaw, so we were talking for about 3 hours. During all that time Faith (that's the girl who gives me my dancing lessons and who came up with me to Jones's studio) was in the other living room and apparently dancing with John and becoming quite friendly with him. Faith came out and started to tell me of the very charming man she had been dancing with and it seemed so strange that he seemed to be asking her questions that more or less had a bearing on my activities. I then told her that that was John (I had told her all about him and how we had quarreled) and she was quite surprised.

About 2:30 in the morning we were all still sitting there in that back room arguing when we heard a knock at the front door. Muschi looked out and saw it was a policeman, so he made me put on my hat and coat and we left the house through the back door. I was terribly frightened. I thought surely the place was being raided and I'd land in jail and there would be a lot of nasty publicity. We stayed away for about 15 minutes, then came back and found out that someone in a house half a mile away had turned in a complaint that we were making too much noise and the police (when they saw that nothing was going on that wasn't right) merely told everybody in a nice way that we had better go home. During that time John managed to find out that Faith and I were going home together and he asked if he couldn't take her home. She accepted and I had to go along naturally, because Muschi had no car and was staying with Jones for the night. John took Faith home first and then we were left alone. I never said a word to him and when we got to my place, he wouldn't let me go in until I had made up with him.

To save myself a lot of unpleasantness, I finally consented to be friends again, but of course I won't. He made me promise him that I'd go out with him Wednesday and to get away, I promised, but I'll manage to be out Wednesday when he calls. I'll be glad to leave California just to lose him. Listen, Irma, if all this stuff I write about my petty little affairs is boring to you, please let me know—otherwise I'll just keep boring you. You see, I have really no one I can write to and say all these things to you without being misunderstood, excepting you and I know that you understand me and even if something doesn't sound quite right, you know and realize that whatever I have done was the right thing regardless of how it sounds or looks.

Sunday before last I went to an afternoon tea at Orselli's studio. Orselli's paintings are beautiful and he has sold quite a number of them. He specializes in portraits and just now he has a commission to do Bebe Daniels's portrait. Orselli is from Florence—he is a very gentle refined type of man and when he talks to you he just keeps you spell bound. His voice is so soft and he speaks beautifully. Mrs. Orselli is very charming too so that all in all I had a delightful afternoon.

So Adolphe Menjou tried to flirt with you! Why didn't you just for fun talk to him? I know it wouldn't have been quite the proper thing to do, but you know if one is proper at all times, one does miss so much. Sometimes you do get into interesting situations by acting on the impulse. Of course, on the other hand, sometimes you become involved in an unpleasant situation, however you have to take a chance at all things—otherwise one's existence becomes somewhat humdrum. You were evidently not very well pleased with your visitor from Australia. That was funny about his wanting to hold your hand in the theatre. Was he good looking or interesting? You don't say much about his personality therefore I assume he was not very interesting.

Before I come East this summer I believe I'll spend about 3 weeks at Valley Ranch in New Mexico. I've worked a year and a half without a vacation and my work is very nerve racking. Perhaps you know what it means to work for people who are very temperamental. The work is not heavy, but it's just the strain of not knowing where you are at most of the time. In the movie business, people just rush about—change their minds a million times about everything and no one seems to know exactly what to do. Everybody acts on the impulse and you are more or less in the air about everything. While I've been able to keep up and have been feeling very well, I think I need a complete rest and to be away from everybody and at Valley Ranch I know I'll get the rest I want. I've also had quite a time all winter going out—taking ballet dancing—and it's impossible to burn the candle at both ends for very long. I've done it now since last September and I feel just a bit exhausted now. I think this has been my happiest year and if I never have another like it, the memory of this year will always be with me and I shall be satisfied to lead a quiet, conventional humdrum existence from now on.

Flo is very busy these days preparing her trousseau. She is planning on getting married the latter part of June. Her fiancé is a very nice fellow and while he has no money, I think in time he will be prosperous. He's been practicing dentistry for about a year and he is establishing himself quite well in his neighborhood.

I'm writing this letter while I'm waiting for Mr. Goldwyn to call me up. He's been up to Frances Marion's home and told me he would call me up to give me a wire. It's now 7:15 and he hasn't called yet. I do hope he will call soon because I'm anxious to get home and rest.

With love to you all, I am
As ever, Valeria

2nd installment

MONDAY—MAY 10TH

Since writing the preceding chapters, I've had a very bad cough that fortunately hasn't developed to the extent that I couldn't work. However, I think I'm run down and I'll just have to quit going out so much and look after myself a bit. Mr. Goldwyn has been very considerate during my indisposition, which came as rather a surprise because his former secretary had told me that unless a girl was well and fit, he could be annoyed with her. However, although I had a pretty bad cough (and still have it) I didn't let it interfere with my work in any way.

Mr. Goldwyn let me off at 3 Saturday and I went straight home and to bed. I met Muschi going home on the car and he asked me to go to Jones' house for Sunday dinner and I accepted. However, around 8 o'clock on Saturday night Muschi called and said the dinner was called off for Sunday but that he and Jones would like me to go with them to the Paris Inn now. I was on the verge of accepting, but my better judgment told me to stay home and take care of my cold, so I refused. Sunday I stayed in bed all morning and then Howard called me up and asked to go to an outdoor symphony concert given by the Artland Club (of which he is a member) and

I went. It was very interesting and I enjoyed it so much. The president of the club is Carrie Jacobs Bond, whom I met and she is a very sweet old woman. After that, we came home and I cooked some steak and French fried potatoes and prepared a salad. My steak was so tough that it was almost impossible to eat it and my potatoes were soggy. The salad was O.K. I don't think Howard was very much impressed with my culinary art, and the only remark he passed was "you are certainly clever in slapping things together on short notice", which of course I considered anything but flattering especially the "slapping things together" part.

John called me up Wednesday and I wasn't in. I made Flo answer the phone and Flo said he sounded very angry. I guess I won't be troubled with him anymore.

3rd installment

Coincidentally, in my rather uncertain attitude towards Muschi, I have come across the following from Shaw's "Man and Superman"

"The true artist will let his wife starve, his children go barefoot, his mother drudge for his living at seventy, sooner than work at anything but his art. To women he is half vivisector, half vampire. He gets into intimate relations with them to study them, to strip the mask of convention from them, to surmise their innermost secrets, knowing that they have the power to rouse his deepest creative energies, to rescue him from his cold reason, to make him see visions and dream dreams, to inspire him, as he calls it. He persuades women that they may do this for their own purpose whilst he really means them to do it for his. He steals the mother's milk and blackens it to make printer's ink to scoff at her and glorify ideal women with. He pretends to spare her the pangs of child bearing so that he may have for himself the tenderness and fostering that belong of right to her children. Since marriage began, the great artist has been known as a bad husband. But he is worse: he is a child robber, a bloodsucker, a hypocrite and a cheat. Perish the race and wither a thousand women if only the sacrifice of them enable him to act Hamlet better, to paint a finer picture, to write a deeper poem, a great play, a profounder philosophy! For mark you, the artists' work is to show us ourselves as we really are. Our minds are nothing but this knowledge of ourselves, and he who adds a job to such knowledge creates new mind as surely as any woman creates new men. In the rage of that creation, he is as ruthless as the woman, as dangerous to her as she to him and as horribly fascinating. Of all struggles, there is none so treacherous and remorseless as the struggle between the artist man and the mother woman. Which shall use up the other? That is the issue between them. And it is all the deadlier because in your romanticist cant, they love one another."

What an indictment against the artist! I showed this to him one night and he smiled saying, "God! How Shaw can show us up—it's almost unbelievable. Shaw must be an artist himself to write a thing like that!"

Personally, I don't believe this applies in all cases, but I do believe Muschi is amply covered by this description.

4th and last installment—May 18, 1926

My dear, I've been having the most hectic time at the studio. Barbara is proving difficult to do and Mr. Goldwyn is on the edge. To add to all his difficulties, Mrs. Goldwyn expects a child in September. I told Mrs. Goldwyn of my intentions to leave and she was very much put out about it and asked if for her sake I wouldn't stay until her baby came. Now, I don't know what to do. My position here demands all my time and energy and I have little or no time left for anything else. My cough is still with me and I'm afraid if I don't take a rest soon, I may seriously injure my health. On the other hand, I want to remain in Goldwyn's good graces, because when I come back from Europe, I know they will be influential in getting me a position.

If you don't hear from me for some time you'll know it's not due to my not wanting to write to you—because I just love to write you, but because I haven't a minute to spare.

With love to you all and hoping to get a nice letter from you soon, I am

As ever, Valeria

ps—It's kind of you to ask me to stay with you and I shall certainly take advantage of your offer providing I won't be too much trouble to your mother.

JUNE 4, 1926

Dear Irma:

Your letter cheered me up so because you seem worried about my health. Out here (at least among my acquaintances) everyone is so blame healthy that no one seems to give a darn whether you're sick or not and therefore one gets very little sympathy. My cough has left me, but I still have a cold in my system and I suppose it won't leave me until I'm able to take a rest.

I told Mr. Goldwyn that I wanted to leave. He was very nice about it, especially when I told him that I would stay until he had found a girl entirely satisfactory to him. As the situation now stands, I don't know definitely when I shall be leaving. I mentioned to Mr.

Goldwyn that while I was in Italy if I came across any story material that I thought suitable to Colman or Banky, I would send it on to his reader in New York. He thought this a splendid idea and told me to send any material I found directly to him and if any of my suggestions were accepted, he would pay me well for them. This, dear Irma, is a splendid opportunity for me, but what I fear is that I haven't the necessary talent to make the most of this opportunity. While I am ambitious, I must admit my mind is very lazy and ideas do not come to me readily. I get ambitious spasmodically—sometimes my mind seems to lie dormant for months and I seem to know absolutely nothing, then I come out of this lethargy and I want to do everything. Unfortunately, these spurts of enthusiasm only last about 2 or 3 weeks and as I grow older, they seem to occur less frequently. How, tell me, how can I accomplish anything when I'm like this? It's a queer world. I have an opportunity of a lifetime—one that thousands of writers would break their necks to have—and here I am with this marvelous opportunity and I haven't the talent or genius to make the most of it. Anyway, when I get to Italy, I'll make a supreme effort to find some material. When I refer to this "marvelous opportunity" I mean that if I had the talent, I could write a story in Italy and send it to Mr. Goldwyn and if it were good, he would accept it, not knowing I had written it. You see, it wouldn't make any difference to him while he's considering the material I submit who wrote it and after he accepts it, I could tell him I wrote it.

You ask what John is. He's an all around promoter—owns several apartment houses in Los Angeles, is interested in a gold mine and dabbles in everything that might make money. He's a good friend of all the artists because when they are hungry, he feeds them, in return for which he is invited to their studio parties and perhaps receives, say a painting from one, a statue from another. However, I'm through with the whole crowd. I've just had enough of them and haven't seen any of them excepting Jones for over a month. Jones called me up about a week ago, brought a friend along and we went to the Paris Inn for dinner and danced away the evening.

I'm glad to know you are all well. Please write me soon,

Love, Valeria

ps. I didn't do much over Memorial Day holiday—just went to the beach on Sunday and Monday. I went to see the first girl I lived with. She has been very sick and I went over and cooked dinner for them which I enjoyed doing. Mr. and Mrs. Goldwyn went on the Hearst yacht to Hearst's ranch. Of course, Marion Davies was in the party.[*]

pps june 5, 1926

Last night around 6:15 my boss turned over his tickets to the Motion Picture Ball given for the Motion Picture Theatre Owner's Convention at the Ambassador to me. So I hustled home—tore about to get someone to take me and finally arrived there. I never saw so many stars gathered under one roof and their clothes were magnificent. I thought my dress was pretty, but it was quite commonplace in comparison. To give you an idea of the gathering, I'll mention just some of the more important stars I saw dancing: John Gilbert, Norma Shearer, Colleen Moore, Norman Kerry, Mary Philbin, Laura La Plante, Raymond

[*]Hearst's "ranch" (a huge estate on more than 250,000 acres) in San Simeon lies on the coast halfway between Los Angeles and San Francisco. Weekend guests rarely arrived by yacht. If they didn't drive themselves, Hearst arranged for cars to drive his guests from the Ambassador Hotel or, if they took the train to San Luis Obispo, they were driven the rest of the way in one of the taxis he kept at the ready. The ranch also had a private airport.

Griffith, Bebe Daniels, Mary Astor, Claire Windsor, Bert Lytell, Harry Langdon, Gertrude Olmstead, Carmel Myers, Richard Barthelmess, Marion Davies, William Boyd, Marion Nixon, May MacAvoy, Bobby Agnew, Walter Pidgeon, Dolores Del Rio, Monte Blue, Dolores Costello, Lou Tellegen and ever so many other lesser stars. However, I didn't enjoy myself so much. Somehow or other I was terribly bored. The entertainment was snappy—almost nude girls did some vulgar dance that disgusted me more than gave me pleasure. The fellow I was with had something on his hip and wanted me to drink. I didn't want to and he therefore thought I was a poor sport. We stayed until about 12:30 and I couldn't stand it any longer, so I left.

JUNE 29, 1926

Dear Irma,

Just a line to let you know I've moved to the Washington Hotel, Culver City. Flo was duly married on Saturday. We had a big party at our house Thursday night and in between being rushed to death at the studio—having a wild crush on one of our actors (he's in Nevada now with company) and all the excitement connected with Flo's marriage—I just don't know where I'm at. I'll be mighty glad when I'm on the train coming east so that I can collect myself. I'm going to drop off on our desert camp for a couple of days because everyone that I know almost is there—but between you and me principally because I will see Gary. I don't expect anything to develop out of this affair—it's just a passing fancy I know.

I am sending you a picture of Rupert Julian—you'd get a great kick seeing him. He looks like one of those dashing villains, but he's as docile as a new born lamb and we are quite good friends (at the studio of course). Am having two new dresses made—a coat and a hat because I'm afraid I won't have much time to spend shopping in New York. It was quite warm today, but fortunately Mr. Goldwyn had a luncheon engagement and I was able to take an hour and a half for lunch. I went over to our outdoor swimming pool and swam for a half hour and feel quite fit now and full of pep. Have to hustle home early if I can because I have to go way over to South Pasadena for my dancing lesson. By the way, at that party at my house, I did some of my dancing. I'm told I did quite well, but of course they were all friends so naturally I don't know how true this is. One thing though, I would never have gotten up and danced—only after one cocktail, why I was quite eager to do it.

With love to all, I am as ever
Valeria

JULY 7, 1926
Dear Irma,

I just received your letter and am writing you immediately because I have an opportune moment.

The new girl came in yesterday—therefore expect to get away in about 2 weeks. I'm very busy darning socks, sewing shoulder straps and wot-nots. I can't afford to throw anything away because when I get to Italy, I won't be in a position to buy things. I've got to watch every cent.

Culver City is an awfully ugly little town and were it not for the fact that I know I won't be here long, I'd hate it. There are a lot of studio people I know at the hotel, so it's not at all lonesome. In fact, I could have what I call a "fast" life and a "merry" one, but you know me, I'm discreet practically all the time. There are about a half dozen fellows here and no girls, so I am rather popular. One or the other take me out to dinner every night, so it's not so bad.

My moment is spent—but will write again. Love to all,

Feeling good again. Presume you are all well. When I get back, will you remind me to tell you of a little episode concerning a Mr. Powell which I cannot write about. It's too good not to repeat to you and it's just "another experience" so far as I'm concerned.

JULY 15, 1926
Dear Irma,

I'm beginning to get a bit excited about my going away, but it's not quite the same feeling I had when I left East and came West. I was so thrilled then—perhaps because I was leaving the known to go into the unknown—whereas coming East I know just what to expect and have no illusions. Things are shaping themselves in such a way that I am rather glad to leave the coast at this time. Flo has gone East. Nancy is all wrapped up in her husband. Ruth works night and day so that we can't plan anything. Another girl, Sybil, that I know is going to San Francisco. I have given up all my artist friends and the only boys I know are ones that I'm not interested in. The one I am interested in is in Nevada and I know that I mean nothing in his young life—hence there is really nothing to look forward to here and I'm a little glad to get away.

I'm craving a change. I hate hotel life and no doubt this is the reason for my gloomy outlook on life just at this moment. I've been here almost a week and I really haven't accomplished anything. I go up to my room and look over my things, use up about 20 minutes deciding what I should do first and, after I've decided, I begin to get lonesome and then look someone I know up at the hotel and the result is that my work is left undone.

Culver City is such an ugly little town and outside of a lot of fast roadhouses, cafes and nightclubs, there is absolutely nothing else one can do here or go to. I went to one of these places Monday night with one of the boys at the hotel and this is one of the experiences I want to tell you about that I referred to in my letter the other day about Mr. Powell.

Nearly everyone at the hotel are studio people—therefore the main topic of conversation is pictures and scandal—gossip about producers, directors, actors, etc. No one can talk of anything else and I'm just fed up listening to the terrible stories I hear about this one and that one. I am beginning to feel that there is something materially wrong with me—at least after hearing what others do and how they live. I thought I was very broadminded, but this crowd is leaps and bounds ahead of me and I feel absolutely like a prim old maid, which I suppose I am in their eyes. I find that no one respects a person for his or her virtues. I find people with the loosest moral codes and almost dishonest in their dealing are looked up to and respected. On the other hand, the one who realizes his moral obligations and duties and is respectable is laughed at and scoffingly called "the virtuous poor". It is disgusting and I wonder if conditions are like this all over.

Just before Mr. Colman went to Nevada on location, I told him what an ardent admirer you were of his and said that if he autographed a special picture to you personally, I know you would appreciate it. He put your name in his book and today I received the enclosed picture for you.

My plans now (I think this is definite) are that I shall leave Los Angeles July 22nd, stay in San Francisco all day, leave San Francisco that night for Camp—will leave Camp about the 27th stopping at Youngstown, Ohio to see Flo for a day so that I ought to arrive in New York about the 3rd of August. I intend staying in New York until about the first of September so that even if you are away on your vacation when I arrive, I'll still have plenty of time to chat with you before I leave for Italy.

Do you know that boy I raved to you about, Gary Cooper? Well I raved so much about him to Mr. Goldwyn, Mrs. Goldwyn and Frances Marion and our casting agent—and in fact to anyone who would listen to me—that Mr. Goldwyn finally wired to camp and asked our manager to sign him up under a five year contract. I was happy that he did this. Of course, this only makes the rift between us wider because he wouldn't have a thought for me since he is now on the road to bigger things, but I am happy anyway and I shall always cherish the thought that I helped him.

Barbara Worth is developing into a marvelous picture and I am sorry in a way that I can't see it through to the finish. Also Fitz is starting in about 2 weeks here on this lot on "Beauty and the Beast". Fitz was surprised when I told him I was leaving and was sorry I wouldn't be here while he was here. Fitz is awfully nice to me, a real good friend, and seems to take an interest in my welfare, therefore I am sorry that I won't see him. His picture, "The Son of the Sheik", is a tremendous success here in Los Angeles. Vilma is wonderful in it, so is Rudy. "Beauty and the Beast" is the last picture he will make for Mr. Goldwyn as he has signed a two year contract with First National. Can you imagine it, with First National, Fitz will get a salary of $5,000 a week for two years. He's just completed a beautiful home in Beverly Hills and I think he is going to be married to Florence Vidor very shortly. Some people are fortunate!

With love to you all, I am
As ever, Valeria

As the years passed, more and more people claimed credit for "discovering" Gary Cooper, the twenty-four-year-old son of a Montana judge who caught Valeria's eye. Still, almost everyone's versions contain a mention of his being "the boyfriend" of Goldwyn's secretary as the way he came to their attention. According to Henry King, he spotted Cooper's abilities right away and had to convince Goldwyn, but Hedda Hopper told the story that Cooper was so much Frances Marion's type (she had a lifelong appreciation of tall, good-looking men) that after Valeria's urging that she take a look at the 6-foot, 3-inch Cooper, Frances then "gave him a second look and as she went through the door, even risked a third."

Marion remembered that neither King nor Goldwyn was impressed at first because they found him to be a "gaunt, slow-moving, self-conscious young man with irregular features." She cajoled them into screening Cooper's test reel to an audience made up of the United Studios' secretaries, and it was the immediate response from the women's collective libidos that convinced them to hire him. Cooper was promoted into the featured role of Abe Lee in *The Winning of Barbara Worth* after the actor originally cast for the part, Harold Goodwin, was held up in an Ernst Lubitsch film running over schedule at Warner Brothers.

Even during the shooting of *Barbara Worth*, it became obvious that the camera loved Cooper. Watching the daily rushes, Marion realized he was going to steal the picture if they left his character as the man who rides for twenty-four hours straight to save the town. She rewrote the scene so that Cooper is injured early in their ride and Colman alone arrives with the money as the undisputed hero of the film.

As Valeria writes, Goldwyn did indeed try to put Cooper under contract before *Barbara Worth* was released, but negotiations faltered when, according to Frances Marion, Goldwyn offered him a contract at $65 a week, rising to $750 a week after six years. Cooper held out for $1,000 for the final year, but Sam refused, saying, "I don't think any kid is worth a thousand a week." Cooper signed with Paramount instead and was cast in *It* opposite Clara Bow, who took an offscreen interest in him as well.

Frances Marion looked back and said she didn't know if she "felt sorrier for Sam Goldwyn for losing a star or his secretary for losing a boyfriend."

JULY 20, 1926

Dear Irma,

This has been one of the happiest days of my life, therefore I must write to you. Miss Marion sent her car down to my hotel to bring me to her home to have lunch with her. I was so thrilled! Miss Marion and I spent the whole afternoon together and she was so affectionate towards me. She has asked me to write to her in the form of a diary everything I see in Italy and about the peasants and their ways because she may possibly publish it! Not only that, but before I come back, I am to notify her about 2 months in advance and if her own secretary is sufficiently well known to go on as a scenario writer, she is going to take me and develop me into a scenario writer and I am to live with her. Irma—it seems impossible I of all people should have won her confidence and regard to such an extent that Miss Marion, the dean and peer of scenario writers, should want me as her protégé! Good God, if only I can be worthy of it and that I may never disappoint her.* Thanks for the invitation to go to Bermuda with you. I would be delighted to go, but my funds really won't permit it. I am so anxious to see you.

Love, Valeria

JULY 22, 1926

To whom it may concern:

Miss Belletti has been working for me in the capacity of private secretary for the past two years. Had it not been for the fact that she desired to leave my employ in order to join her father who is in Rome, I would have been delighted to have her continue with me, as I have always found her honest, industrious and very capable and consider her the best secretary I have had in 15 years. I am sure that Miss Belletti will be an asset to anyone who may be fortunate in securing her services.

Samuel Goldwyn [huge signature]

---

*Frances Marion was well known for being generous to a fault; Adela Rogers St. Johns called her a one-woman employment office because she was on the phone so often trying to find work for her friends. She wrote one of the first film textbooks, *How to Write and Sell Film Stories*, and hosted seminars in her home for film students and arranged internships for them at the studios. Frances joked about her own proclivities, referring to one snub by saying, "I don't know why she is mad at me. I haven't done anything for her lately."

Because she was back east and visiting with Irma at the time, we don't have Valeria's reaction to the death of Rudolph Valentino on August 23, 1926. He was in New York for the premiere of *The Son of the Sheik* and died there at the age of thirty-one from a massive infection that followed his hospitalization for a perforated ulcer. Over 100,000 people walked past his casket in New York, the train that carried his body back to California was swarmed at every stop, and his funeral in Los Angeles caused such a mob scene that streets were blocked off and schools were closed. United Artists rushed *The Son of the Sheik* into general release, where it made a fortune at the box office.

After two weeks in New York, Valeria boarded the Cunard line's ship *Berengaria* on Wednesday, September 1, 1926. Landing at Cherbourg, Valeria took the train to Paris and arrived that night; an hour later, she boarded the train that would take twenty-four hours to reach Ventimiglia, Italy, just across the French border. After spending the night in that small town on the Mediterranean coast, she cabled her father at Perinaldo, a hill town about an hour and a half inland, that she had finally arrived.

SEPTEMBER 12, 1926

Dear Irma,

After a most enjoyable trip to Italy, the end of my journey has been far from pleasant. When I arrived at Ventimiglia I wired my father at Perinaldo to come for me. About an hour later, the telegraph office sent for me and told me the wire was undelivered because my father had died about two months ago. It is useless to tell you how I felt—to find myself in a strange country—not knowing who are my friends and rather short of funds. I immediately left for Perinaldo and am now staying with the people my father lived with. They are very nice to me and try to make me comfortable. Perinaldo is still a 15th century village—everything is very primitive as well as the people. I shall have to stay here until I have everything settled. No doubt you know the red tape of the Italian laws—therefore I suppose I shall have to stay here for some time. I shall do some writing from here (there's an abundance of material hereabouts) and for diversion shall take weekend trips to Monte Carlo and Cannes. These places are about 2 hours bus ride from this village and the fare is only 5 francs each way. However, at the present time I cannot do anything because I came to Italy with a limited amount of money, expecting to meet my father whom I would have asked for a loan until the first of January when I made arrangements with the bank in America to send me money. As I don't know when I shall be able to draw on the money which I will inherit from my father, could you be so kind as to loan me $100 until the first of the year? I am approaching you for this loan because I recall when I left America you offered to loan me some money if I needed it. If it is possible for you to do this, I would suggest you draw a draft at the Commercial Bank because this bank has a branch office at Ventimiglia in Italy.

I am told my father was so happy at the thought of seeing me that he kept talking to everyone in the village about me. About a week after he received my letter, he had a stroke. The stroke affected only one side of his body and while everybody thought he could live long enough to see me, he was sure that he would die before I arrived. For eight days all he kept saying was, "Non la vede piu la mia Valeria" and then died with my name on his lips. I am told that whenever he received a letter from me, he carried it about and showed it to everybody and would say "Isn't it wonderful to be called 'padre'." You see, I used to address my letters "Cara padre". I cannot write much more because my pen point is out of commission and I cannot get another until I go to Ventimiglia.

Your letters will be so appreciated here in this other world—so please write soon.

Love, Valeria

My address is:

> Via Genova N4
> Ventimiglia per Perinaldo
> Provincia Imperiia, Italia

OCTOBER 13, 1926
Dear Irma,

I am still here at Perinaldo and have just gotten over quite a sick spell. I suppose the fact that I couldn't get my proper sleep weakened my system and caught cold which resulted in an attack of bronchitis and have been laid up for about a week. Today is really the first day that I feel a bit better; before I got sick I had had to do a lot of running around on account of settling my father's affairs and the way things are done here in Italy would make anyone sick—I became so nervous and excited on account of having to hang around in first one town hall and then another. However, I suppose this nervousness was merely a foreboding of the sickness coming on. I had to take 4 men from Perinaldo to Bordighera before the Judge in order to prove that I am my father's sole heir. I of course had to buy their dinners and I ate with them. Well, everything went on splendidly until they started to drink and then I left the 4 of them because they were getting quite drunk—you see I was paying for the wine and naturally they kept on getting one bottle after another and I couldn't very well stop it because they had been kind enough to swear to the fact that I was my father's daughter and they knew there was no other heir. After I left them I went to Ventimiglia. Some old man on the street car tried to flirt with me and followed me all along the walk near the water—he spoke to me and I was furious. I got rid of him and then 3 or 4 fellows about 17 passed by and started smacking their lips—well after that happened I was fit to be tied. When I got to Perinaldo that night I took sick.

Today being my first day up, I was invited to visit some people who live just a few houses up the road. While I hardly felt well enough to go visiting, I thought the change of atmosphere would benefit me—you see these people are considered the Elite of Perinaldo and have really a very nice house, so I went. There I met the "400" of Perinaldo which includes the school teacher, the mayor of the town and his wife; a young man who owns the only automobile in Perinaldo and another fellow who is merely vacationing here but is a doctor from San Remo. I enjoyed the visit very much as a consequence I have a place where I can go for my baths. These people have a bathroom with running water in the house (the only house in Perinaldo with such a luxury) and they told me to come there any time I wanted to take a bath.

The first two weeks I arrived here I used to go to Ventimiglia every other day swimming. The weather was wonderful and I thought I might just as well take advantage of it because I knew it wouldn't last very much longer. There I met a very charming fellow, Giglio Rostand. Of course he is one of these typical Italians who love the life of ease—but he doesn't waste his time entirely—you see he is a playwright and poet. He used to meet me at Ventimiglia and we always spent the day together. He was very interesting and I used to love to sit near the sea (it resembles the water near Catalina Island) and listen to his poetry and plays. Through him I also met his cousin who is also very elegant and another chap who spent a year in London and could therefore speak English quite well. However, the friendship between Giglio and myself is broken—the people of Ventimiglia and Perinaldo all knew that we saw each other and my dear the natives had me married to him already. He indirectly proposed to me but I knew that it isn't because he really loves me but because he thinks I am immensely wealthy that he would like to marry me. Therefore under the circumstances I have thought it best not to meet him anymore.

How are you all and what have you been doing—anything exciting? Do write to me soon.

Love, Valeria

The Perinaldo post master has just been here to deliver your letter and I thank you for the draft. Your letter was so comforting and I feel much happier after having read it. It is a wonderful thing to have friends like you. As you can never tell what may happen to me, I am sending a note for the money you sent me and I presume it will not inconvenience you any if I do not repay the loan until January. I don't know why the people here did not cable me—I suppose it never occurred to them that it was possible to do such a thing. You have no idea how ignorant the people are here. There is only one thing they are proficient in and that is to slander and talk about each other.

Wedding portrait of Valeria's parents.
Courtesy of Margery Baragona.

Valeria at age 12 in traditional dress.
Courtesy of Margery Baragona.

Valeria's first communion.
Courtesy of Margery Baragona.

Valeria dressed to go
to work in Manhattan,
1916. Courtesy of Margery
Baragona.

"The thrill of thrills."
Valeria and Irma take
off in San Diego.
Courtesy of Margery
Baragona.

Valeria and
Irma outside St.
Catherine's on
Catalina Island.
Courtesy of Margery
Baragona.

Sam Goldwyn with his new wife, Frances, on the left, and his new star, Vilma Banky, on the right. "No doubt by this time you know that Mr. Goldwyn has married Miss Frances Howard. In a way I'm glad because it might make him just a little more gentle and considerate of his secretary" (letter of April 23, 1925). Courtesy of the Samuel Goldwyn Foundation.

"Miss Frances Marion was in today. She is our scenario and continuity writer" (letter of February 27, 1925). Author's collection.

George Fitzmaurice directing Rudolph Valentino and Vilma Banky in *Son of the Sheik*. "Fitz is awfully nice to me, a real good friend, and seems to take an interest in my welfare.... His picture, 'The Son of the Sheik,' is a tremendous success here in Los Angeles. Vilma is wonderful in it, so is Rudy" (letter of July 15, 1926). Courtesy of Bison Archives.

"Mr. Henry King hands me his mail and says 'Here, answer it — I don't care what you say, so long as you're polite in declining everything'" (letter of May 20, 1925). Courtesy of Bison Archives.

"You ought to see
Ronald Colman in
his British uniform
as he appears in
'Dark Angel.' He is
a stunner. My heart
skips a beat every
time he talks to me"
(letter of June 10,
1925).
Courtesy of the Academy
of Motion Picture Arts
and Sciences.

Viola Dana. "I saw them shoot her
death bed scene and then she sat up
and said in a very tough voice: 'Hey
Mame' (that's her maid) 'Gimme a
cigarette'" (letter of May 20, 1925).
Author's collection.

Nita Naldi "is gorgeous. Her beauty just takes your breath away — but what an awakening when she talks — so vulgar and loud" (letter of March 1925). Author's collection.

Corinne Griffith "is very haughty and disdainful. She looks at no one but her dogs and is generally disliked by all" (letter of March 1925). Author's collection.

Aileen Pringle "and the art director at MGM lived together, then for business reasons the art director had to go to New York and this same art director came back from New York with a twenty-year-old girl whom he married in Hollywood and Aileen was the bride's maid — big hearted Aileen. She is noted for her generosity, especially in matters of this kind" (letter of March 10, 1926). Author's collection.

Conrad Nagel "was seated at the next table and seems to be quite a personality, although not so good looking. Has beautiful table manners" (letter of February 27, 1925). Author's collection.

"Saw Lewis Stone today. He's adorable with his make up on. I don't know how he looks without it. No doubt like any ordinary middle aged man" (letter of February 27, 1925).
Author's collection.

"Huntley Gordon is still on the lot and very distinguished looking. He surely has it all over these young sheiks" (letter of February 2, 1926).
Author's collection.

"Ran into Thomas Meighan on the lot, who is really good looking. Beautiful blue-black wavy hair, sunburned, twinkling eyes, etc." (letter of February 27, 1925). [He] makes $10,000 a week" (letter of September 20, 1925). Author's collection.

"I saw Constance Talmadge today having her hair dried on the porch right next to my office. I was so surprised to see she had blonde hair" (letter of April 8, 1925). Author's collection.

"Marion Davies had quite a blow out last week for the opening of her new picture 'Zander the Great.' Everybody who is somebody in the movie industry was there" (letter of March 10, 1926). Author's collection.

"As for my boss, Mr. Samuel Goldwyn, I've heard so much about him that there is little I can say that is nice. . . . I suppose as his secretary, I should not say anything more about his personal affairs, so I'll tell you about all the other scandals but his" (letter of February 27, 1925). Courtesy of the Academy of Motion Picture Arts and Sciences.

"Alice Joyce, who is playing the part of Mrs. Morrison, is beautiful—she is so dignified. Owen Moore was her former husband [and before that, the husband of Mary Pickford]. Miss Joyce's present husband is James Regan—he's quite distinguished looking and comes every night to take her home" (letter of July 14, 1925). Author's collection.

"Elinor Glyn was to the studio to lunch with Mr. Goldwyn. She's very eccentric—wore a pale lavender dress and hat—has a bright red wig and her face is powdered very white—her eyes are blackened and her lips are straight slits of red. Isn't it killing to think she makes a fortune out of such stories" (letter of July 1925). Courtesy of the Academy of Motion Picture Arts and Sciences.

Valeria hiking with Nancy on
Mount Lowe, 1925.
Courtesy of Margery Baragona.

Valeria at the beach with her "Bohemian friends." Courtesy of Margery Baragona.

Sam Goldwyn, Lois Moran, and Henry King in front of Valeria's office on the United Studios lot. Courtesy of Bison Archives.

Belle Bennett and Lois Moran in a scene from *Stella Dallas.* "The cast for 'Stella Dallas' is nearly completed. Belle Bennett will play Stella; . . . and Lois Moran (that's the 16-year-old girl Mr. Goldwyn brought from Paris) will play Laurel" (letter of June 6, 1925). Courtesy of the Academy of Motion Picture Arts and Sciences.

Pola Negri. "After her affair with Chaplin cooled off and Rod La Rocque was bewitched, if she didn't have the audacity to bring Rod to the very same apartment — in fact in the very same bed — where she had just previously had Chaplin. That, in my judgment, was unpardonable — the least she could have done was to have Rod in a different suite of rooms. However, that is Pola for you" (letter of March 10, 1926). Author's collection.

Rudolph Valentino, bidding goodbye to Joe Schenck and his wife, Norma Talmadge, at the train station in New York, just weeks before Valentino's death. Courtesy of the Museum of Modern Art.

Valeria on the beach. Courtesy of Margery Baragona.

Gary Cooper. "Do you know that boy I raved to you about, Gary Cooper? Well I raved so much about him to Mr. Goldwyn, Mrs. Goldwyn and Frances Marion and our casting agent — and in fact to anyone who would listen to me — that Mr. Goldwyn finally wired to camp and asked our manager to sign him up" (letter of July 15, 1926). Author's collection.

Valeria in Ventimiglia, Italy.
Courtesy of Margery Baragona.

Valeria (far left) with "the girls from the Langner office," New York, 1927. Courtesy of Margery Baragona.

Kathy, Valeria, Flo, and Nancy (left to right), 1928. Courtesy of Margery Baragona.

Valeria and "the girls from the studio at the beach in Santa Monica," 1929. Courtesy of Margery Baragona.

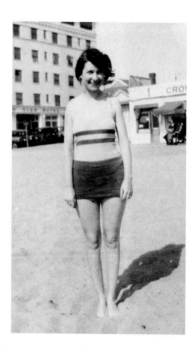

Valeria at the Santa
Monica beach, 1929.
Courtesy of Margery Baragona.

"Do you remember Culver City? The DeMille Studios is a big white colonial mansion. There is a negro in uniform standing outside the door and every morning when our car pulls up in front of the studio, he runs down the steps, opens the door, runs up ahead of me and opens the door in the building and boughs [sic]. Never had such service in my life" (letter of March 31, 1926). Courtesy of Bison Archives.

DeMille directing a scene from *The Godless Girl*. Courtesy of the Academy of Motion Picture Arts and Sciences.

Cecil B. DeMille and his screenwriter Jeanie Macpherson. "I was quite thrilled the other day when I was sent to Miss Jeanie Macpherson who dictated some scenes on 'The Godless Girl' which DeMille is going to direct himself" (letter of December 14, 1927). Courtesy of the Academy of Motion Picture Arts and Sciences.

"The hard boiled eggs on this lot is Phyllis Haver and she sure is hard — disgustingly so" (letter of January 31, 1928). Author's collection.

"Gloria Swanson is making a picture on our lot called 'Queen Kelly' with Von Stroheim directing. I have only seen Gloria once. She seems quite friendly and I was surprised to see that her hair wasn't dark. It's quite a light brown. Somehow or other I had the idea she was very dark" (letter of January 19, 1929).
Author's collection.

Valeria and Tony Baragona, 1941
Courtesy of Margery Baragona.

Valeria and Tony Jr., 1935.
Courtesy of Margery Baragona.

Valeria with her paintings in
Santa Barbara in the early
1950s. Courtesy of
Margery Baragona.

Dear Irma,

I received your card today and clippings and you can't realize how pleased I was to receive them.

Things are still the same as before, but I believe that within a week everything will be settled and then I shall be able to get away from Perinaldo. My health is as before and I am beginning to feel a bit happier.

There are more reasons than one why I want to get away from Perinaldo. One reason is Berto (the fellow with the car that I told you about in my last letter). Last Sunday Berto invited me to go riding with him. We left Perinaldo about 9 in the morning and we stopped at Ventimiglia because Berto wanted to stop there and change his clothes. You see his home is in Ventimiglia but he stays in Perinaldo for the summer. He stopped the car in front of this store (a few blocks from his home) and in front of this store there were two girls seated. I got out of the car to walk around and I noticed one of the girls rise from her chair quickly, throwing the chair down and run after Berto. And then an awful scene took place—the girl talked loudly and said some awful things to him right in the street. I walked on as if nothing happened but I knew of course that something was wrong. However, I waited for Berto and then we drove on. We drove all along the Riviera—it was a beautiful day and I did enjoy the ride although Berto is awfully dull. We stopped at San Remo for dinner and got back to Perinaldo about 7. The next day I went to Ventimiglia in the bus and the driver told me that I had better be careful because everybody knew I had been out with Berto and that this girl in Ventimiglia had lived with Berto 5 years and then he had put her out—however, she left on condition that he does not go with any other women; so you see what a cad Berto was to deliberately take me in front of her home. Berto has a terrible reputation and now that I have been seen with him, why my reputation is gone too. People are horribly narrow minded here and it seems that everything I do is wrong. For instance I went hiking one day in my knickers and everybody was horrified. When I went bathing I was told that if it weren't for the fact that there were few people on the beach that the women would have driven me away because they considered my suit indecent.

And another thing is Rostand. I told you that I had decided not to see him anymore—but after not seeing him for about 2 weeks I just craved someone to talk to intelligently; therefore I weakened and I met him again and have been meeting him every other day. He is an awfully decent chap and our friendship is purely platonic. Now it develops that Rostand is not a Fascist and in view of this all his actions are viewed with suspicion. On account of my being seen with him so much, the Fascisti have decided that I have come from America and am plotting with Rostand against the Fascisti and a meeting of the Fascisti was called to investigate my doings and to watch me. Can you imagine anything so stupid? I have already been warned not to be seen with him anymore, but I'll be da-ned if I'm going to let any political party tell me—an American—who I can talk with and who I can't.

I told Rostand about this and he frankly admitted to me that if it weren't for the fact that he had a medal for valor during the war and his uncle was an admiral in the Italian navy, he would have been in prison long ago. He feels terrible to think that I have been placed in such a position on account of him and yesterday (we spent the whole day together way up on top of a mountain over looking the Mediterranean; outside an old abandoned fort between France and Italy). Rostand told me he had written to a friend in Nice and just as soon as he could make the necessary arrangements, he was going to escape to France.

Two days ago I met a Giovanni Maccario who is a professor of Belle Lettres at the University in Rome. He is spending 3 weeks in the mountains on a hunting trip. The bus driver introduced him to me and I spent the other day with him at Bordighera. He is very interesting but a little too effeminate to suit me. Tomorrow I have a date to meet him at the "Chiesa della Madonna" which is a little chapel about a 1/2 mile from Perinaldo. We are going hunting together and he is bringing lunch for us both and his Kodak. I feel rather fortunate in having met him because when I go to Rome I'll have some one to show me about. He is very well learned—knows Greek and Latin and speaks Italian beautifully and French also. While he is quite an important person and he does seem to be very much interested in me, I must confess I like Rostand much better. I really can't understand myself—Rostand almost ignores me since he knows that I wouldn't consider marriage and I don't believe he has ever called me by my first name or said anything complimentary to me—he just treats me as if I were another man—reads his plays and poetry to me—talks about plays of other authors but never anything personal. His indifference is rather interesting and I am wondering how long it will keep up. On the other hand Maccario, whom I know only two days, already calls me by my first name, is very attentive and is so anxious to please me. Now why I shouldn't like Maccario better than Rostand is a mystery to me. No doubt my going on a hunting trip with a man will give Perinaldo more material for gossip and all the women will have a delightful time talking about me. Irma, if you ever want to be the center of attraction, just come to a small town in Italy and you will find no matter what you do, everybody will be discussing you and watching every move you make. How I hate this town! I can't understand how my father could have lived here for a year. I suppose you have been wondering why I don't leave now that I've received your draft, but you see the bank at Ventimiglia hasn't received a notice from the bank in America and they can't pay me the money until this notice is received. No doubt it will reach the bank some day this week and I can assure you that just as soon as I get the money, I shall clear out of Perinaldo.

I am now reading Byron and have come across the following which I think you will appreciate:

> They say that Hope is happiness;
> But genuine love must prize the past
> And Memory wakes the thoughts that bless
> They rose the first—they set the last;
>
> And all that Memory loves the most
> Was once our only Hope to be,
> And all that Hope adored and lost
> Hath melted into memory.
>
> Alas! The delusion is all:
> The future cheats us from afar,
> Nor can we be what we recall,
> Nor dare we think on what we are.

I am also reading Tolstoy's "Resurrection" in Italian, but am not enjoying it so much because I have to stop so often to look up the meaning of various words. However, I think this is a good way of learning Italian.

Hoping you are all well and with love to you and your family I am

As ever,
Valeria

NOVEMBER 27, 1926

Dear Irma,

It's ages since I've heard from you and I am quite worried about you. Are you ill?

I am still at Bordighera and am having a delightful time. Four wealthy English women who are stopping at the same hotel as I am have been extremely kind to me and they insist on taking me around with them. They go to a Tea-Dansant every afternoon and they have introduced me to a number of other English people at these functions. I've met a Colonel Peacock who is quite interesting and a number of Sirs and Ladys whose names I've forgotten. The winter colony here is quite exclusive and there are so many titled people—Counts and Countesses from Germany, Belgium and Hungary—Barons and Baronesses from all over and there are about 4 or 5 Princes and Princesses and then of course there are any number of Sirs and Ladys. I feel just a little out of my element, but I am just myself and as I am not easily flustered, no one suspects I'm only a poor honest working girl. However, this will be my last week here and then I have to go on to Turin. I've settled everything here and as it is very expensive to live here, I must of course go, but I must admit I am rather loathe to leave my present pleasant and happy surroundings.

The English women I referred to above have invited me to visit them in London so before returning to America I shall stop in London for about a week. After I've settled everything in Turin, I am retuning to the Riviera but I shall go to Nice in France so that I can learn some French. My Italian is not so good but I manage to make myself understood and I'd like to know as much French as I do Italian.

Since I've been in Bordighera I've had no trouble with Fascisti—in fact two Fascisti officers who drop in to Tea every day have been dancing with me and are extremely friendly. My friend Giglio Rostand didn't come to see me for 2 weeks after I came to Bordighera—I felt horribly lonesome those 2 weeks and couldn't imagine what I had done that kept him away so long. However, he now visits me about every other day and everything is all right. He expects to be able to get away to France shortly and when I go to Nice I expect he will be there.

To be frank with you, I must admit that I am quite tired of Italy—perhaps it's due to the weather. We have had a continual downpour for over a month and it's beginning to get on my nerves. It's rain, rain, rain, rain every day and night—I've never longed for Sunny California as I have been for the last month. Of course I feel much happier here in Bordighera than I did in Perinaldo—but I was perfectly miserable there.

I sincerely hope there is nothing wrong in your household which has prevented you from writing to me and that you yourself are well.

With love to all,
I am, as ever
Valeria

JANUARY 3, 1927

Dear Irma,

I received your letter and clippings for which I thank you. It was all news to me because outside of receiving the Los Angeles clippings on Barbara Worth from one of the girls at the studio, I haven't seen a New York paper since I have been in Italy.

The 5th of December I left Bordighera for Turin where I stayed 2 weeks in order to attend to the transfer of some bonds my father had in a bank there. I had a very nice time there because I met a fellow who took me to theatres, cafes and dances. I left Turin on December 20th for Mombercelli where my cousins from New York have a villa. The day after I arrived at my cousins I was taken ill with bronchitis and asthma and have been in bed until yesterday. It's taking an awfully long time for me to get better and there is one thing I am now convinced of and that is that I cannot possibly live in a cold climate. I suffered so much that all I am waiting for is the summer so that I can return to the United States and go to Los Angeles. I cannot go out yet for 2 weeks as the doctor is afraid I shall get pneumonia, but just as soon as I can, I am going back to the Riviera for the winter. Things are awfully expensive here so that my money is going fast and when there is nothing coming in, it won't be long before I will have spent all my money and without pleasure.

Hoping you are well and with love to you all, I am

As Ever,
Valeria

PS Please continue to write me at my Perinaldo address

JANUARY 9, 1927
Dear Irma,

I just received your nice long letter of the 19th which I enjoyed so much. Several days ago I wrote you and you know that I have been very ill. I am feeling much better, but you know that after one has been in bed for 2 weeks, it takes quite some time to recover and I doubt whether I shall be able to go out of the house for another ten days.

I hear from my English friends from Bordighera often and they are very anxious that I return. I had planned on going to the French Riviera just as soon as I was able to travel but since these people are so friendly towards me, perhaps it would be a better plan than if I spent the rest of the winter in Bordighera.

So far I have done nothing in Italy. All my ambition is gone. I think a person must be amongst "doers" in order to accomplish anything and as you know Italy is not a country that inspires one to work. Then my health has been miserable and I am just drifting. I am making notes and I hope when I return to Hollywood I will be able to draw on my memory for material. My only thought now is to get well and I am going to just enjoy myself whenever I have the opportunity.

So sorry you did not meet Vilma. However, if you come to Hollywood and I am still in the movie colony, I'll see to it that you get a personal introduction. I received a lovely letter from Mrs. Goldwyn telling me about her baby and inviting me to be sure to visit her when I return to Hollywood, providing of course that I do return. I've heard from everybody at the studio—such cheering notes and all asking me to come back soon. Really, Irma, people may say what they want about studio people—but once they take to a person, you can surely count on their staunch support and they are friendly.

Frances Marion is expecting a child so I suppose she has very little time to write to me. I doubt whether she is well because she was not too well when I left Hollywood. I wrote her several times but received no answer so I have thought it best under the circumstances not to annoy her with letters.

How lucky of you to have met someone who knows George Gray Barnard and to have an opportunity of visiting The Cloisters.

My friend from Turin has written me several times and from the tone of his letters, I am afraid he is taking things rather seriously. He is leaving Turin tomorrow for Florence where he works for his uncle who has an art gallery and antique shop. He wants me to be sure to visit Florence in the Spring and has promised to take me through all the art galleries and museums. Since he's in that business himself he naturally knows a lot about it and I am therefore looking forward to my visit to Florence. My friend's name is Vittorio Castellano and I rather like him. He is not very tall but after all, appearance means very little when a person is interesting. I hear from Giglio but I'd rather lost interest in him since I've met Vittorio. Giglio is a dreamer and I don't really think he cares to work—whereas Vittorio is very ambitious and after all, men who have an object in life are more interesting—don't you think so?

Do write me all about The Cloisters and your friend—and here's luck—may he prove to be "the friend" you have been looking for all your life. You can always reach me by writing to Perinaldo and please write to me frequently because I do worry when I don't hear from you.

With love to all, I am

As ever,
Valeria

FEB. 2, 1927

Dear Irma,

I am still with my cousins at Mombercelli and haven't been out of the house yet! Surely, I am having a hard time of it and I'm wondering why I have to suffer so. While I've been up in my room for over a month, I've been pondering and pondering why some mortals must struggle so for everything. One must indeed make the most of our moments of happiness because one never knows just what the next moment holds for us. Perhaps there's a reason for it all, but who knows?

How is everything with you?

If I can stay up 3 days without getting an attack of asthma, I am going to Bordighera and I think once there, I will improve.

I am enclosing a check for the amount you loaned me plus interest and I want to thank you again for your kindness.

With love to all, I am
As ever,
Valeria

FEB. 23, 1927

Dear Irma,

I just received your letter and clippings. Thanks so much.

After being in bed a month I finally got over my bronchitis and I left immediately for Bordighera and Perinaldo where I was going to pack my trunk which I had left in Perinaldo with the intention of returning immediately to America. However, when I got to Bordighera one of my English friends asked me if I wouldn't accompany her daughter who is crippled to Rome and stay there a week with her. As I wanted to see Rome before returning I readily consented. My expenses are being paid and we are stopping at a lovely hotel and of course we ride in a carriage whenever outdoors. Such luxury! However, I can enjoy it because I'm not paying for it.

We arrived here last night and today we have been through the Capitolino museum. It's perfectly wonderful and I do regret that I can't stay longer.

By the way, the head waiter here at the hotel thinks my profession is "damaselle de compania" and doesn't know I am American and returning to America very soon. In the circumstances he has been trying to get me to go with him to the theater and to see the Forum by moonlight. I told him I couldn't because my mistress demands all my time. He thinks it's awful that I should be a slave to her and give her all my time—he is so sympathetic.

Next Monday, I leave for Naples and on March 2 I am sailing on the Conte Biancamano. I have already booked my passage and I am thrilled at the thought of getting back.

I have just received a letter from my friend Rostand. One of his plays has won some sort of prize or other and he is now commissioned to write a play and has written to me to help him with a theme which we have discussed when I had last seen him in Ventimiglia.

When I return I have some very amusing letters from another fellow I met in Turin. I'll tell you all about it when I see you because it is rather a long story.

I hope to return to Italy some time in the future, but when I come again I want someone with me. It is very unpleasant for a girl to travel alone here and it's mostly for this reason that I haven't enjoyed parts of my trip.

Things are quite expensive here in Italy and for this reason I haven't bought any clothes whatsoever here outside of a pair of shoes that I paid 120 lire for and which in America would cost about $5 because they are not at all stylish or chic.

I shall be so glad to see you all again and to be back again in America.

Love to all, Valeria

After six months abroad, Valeria returned to America in mid-March 1927. There was the house in West New York to come home to as well as her aunt, her cousins, and, of course, Irma. One change was that the house next door had been sold and the new neighbors were the Baragona family. They had five children, and the eldest, Tony, was working in New York for John Hancock Insurance. He was only twenty-two (Valeria was twenty-eight), but he was mature beyond his years; in addition to helping support his family, he had already purchased a small house for himself.

Tony was immediately attracted to Valeria, and she was interested enough to stay around for a while. She took a secretarial job with the Palisades Park office in downtown New York for the summer, but there was no way she was going to live through another eastern winter. She missed California — the climate, the excitement of the studios, and her friends. When Tony said he would save his money and follow her within the year, she wasn't about to dissuade him. She would see how she felt about him from a distance; after all, it was nice to have a man in reserve in case she didn't meet someone else. Once again, Valeria packed her bags and headed west, unsure of what changes she would find after being gone for more than a year. And once again, it was to Irma that Valeria turned to share her thoughts and report her activities.

....

OCTOBER 20, 1927

Dear Irma,

I delayed writing to you because I wanted to get a job first and then write, but as I am still unemployed and no prospects ahead I felt I should write regardless.

I have seen all my old friends and everybody has been wonderful to me, but there are just no openings anywhere and I shall just have to wait until there is one. In the meantime Jimmie and Jack have arrived with their car and I have been showing them all the interesting spots. We've been to Catalina for two days, San Diego and Tia Juana for four days. I went to the races but lost $2.50. Played roulette and lost—played the money machines and lost—in fact luck is just against me it seems, but I'm not worried. I feel ever so much better than in N.Y. and that's something to be thankful for. The weather is simply marvelous—so warm and sunshiny. We've had only one cloudy day since I've been here.

I've taken an apartment to myself until I know where I shall be working. If I get something in Culver City, I'll live with Helen and, if in Hollywood, with another girl I know.

Tomorrow I am going to really make an earnest effort to get a job and if I can't get anything at the studios I'll go downtown Los Angeles in some law office temporarily.

Hoping you are well and with love to you, your mother and Isabella, I am

Sincerely, Valeria

1522 4/5 Reid St.
Los Angeles

NOVEMBER, 1927
WEDNESDAY AFTERNOON
Dear Irma:

I'm back at work for DeMille. It's not just the sort of work I want, but I'm keeping in touch with the industry and that counts a lot. I'm in the script and scenario department and I have to take dictation from the various writers. This is my second day here, but so far I've only been typing a story, "My Country," featuring Rudolph Schildkraut. Furthermore, it's only temporary work, so I may be laid off any time. Get $30 per week. The work is not at all nerve racking and I don't have to work so very hard. I saw Frances Marion yesterday and she was very nice to me. She has spoken to the head of the scenario department of Metro Goldwyn Mayer and the first opening I am sure I will get. I think if I get in with MGM and with Frances Marion on the lot, I will have a fine opportunity for working myself up. You see I will come in contact with all the writers and will have a chance of studying their technique when working for them. MGM start their girls at $25 per week and in six months increase their salary to $27.50 and at the end of the year, a girl (if ambitious and intelligent) is usually assigned to some writer as secretary and the salary ranges from $35.00 to $50.00. While this is not as much as I would get as a secretary to an executive, I think it will be better because I won't have to devote all my time to one man and be so exhausted at the end of the day that I don't want to do anything else but rest.

It seems good to be back in a studio—it is so much better than working in an office downtown. The room I am working in now is opposite one of the stages, and I have Leatrice Joy, William Boyd, Joseph Schildkraut pass by. The sun is shining in all over and the windows are wide open. Against the stage opposite my window is a little patch of grass and some flowers—three perfectly gorgeous calla lilies are in bloom. On the other side is the mill and I hear the saws buzzing all day long (this is the carpenter shop on the lot).

I haven't had any exciting times and I'm just content to lead a quiet life. I don't want to meet that artist crowd again—fortunately they've always called on me when I was out. Sunday I'm invited to a tea in Helen's apartment to meet a chap who works at the studio

(I have already been introduced to him). He is the architect for Goldwyn and wants to go abroad next May and is anxious to talk things over with me and get some ideas from me as to where to go in Italy.

There is a possibility of my going to live with a girl who works over at MGM. She has aspirations to become a writer and she already has a good break. She is assistant to one of the directors so perhaps together we can do something.

Had a very interesting session yesterday afternoon with two writers who are adapting a story for Rod La Rocque called "Hold 'em Yale". They dictated the skeleton of the story in sequence form and I enjoyed doing it very much, even though I had to come back in the evening to work on it.

Jimmie and Jack have a bungalow here in Culver City and since I had to go back to the studio, I went to their place and cooked dinner for all of us and I also invited Helen over. It seemed quite homey for us to be together and I didn't mind cooking. Helen helped me and when we finished, the boys drove me to the studio so that I got out of washing the dishes, for which I was thankful. I don't mind cooking, but I hate to clean up the pots and pans.

I am feeling quite well and I'm glad to be back again. I am anxiously awaiting a letter from you to know how you all are, and with love to you all,

I am,
As ever,
Valeria

Dear Irma,

I received your letter and was glad to hear you are all well.

Things seem to be shaping themselves very well and I feel quite happy. I like my work immensely—am doing just what I wanted to do. As I wrote you before, I am working with three Yale men on a story for Rod La Rocque. One of the writers has asked me if I could work about two nights a week on a story he is working on now on the side and of course I accepted—I'll make about $5.00 a night and that will help a lot. Also I was quite thrilled the other day when I was sent to Miss Jeanie Macpherson* who dictated some scenes on "The Godless Girl" which DeMille is going to direct himself. I also had to do some work for Ernest Pascal who is an author and you no doubt have heard of him. Then I had to work with a director—write titles for a picture and worked in the projection room.

After I started work at DeMille's, the MGM company (at Miss Marion's request) offered me a job in their script department, but I turned it down because I think the job I have at DeMille's is better. I also had an offer as secretary to Gardner Sullivan who is Production manager at United Artists, but I don't want to go into the executive end of the work—I've had enough of that. So you see, things are not as bad as they seemed at first.

*Jeanie Macpherson was DeMille's top screenwriter. A beautiful redhead born in Boston, she had studied opera in Paris before acting on the stage and then in films for D. W. Griffith. DeMille cast her in a film in 1914, and soon she was writing scenarios for him. She had risen in his favor to the point that she and DeMille had adjoining offices and in spite of their long-term affair, there was little talk that he kept her on for any reason but her talent; he had many mistresses but only a few screenwriters.

The people I am boarding with are awfully nice to me—it's like a real home and yet I have all the freedom of a private home of my own. When I want to be with the family, they are only too glad to have me and when I don't want to, I have my own little sitting room aside from my bedroom. Helen lives on the same block and another girl I know, so that in the evening we sometimes get together and play bridge. One night we went to Los Angeles to hear the Florentine Choir—I did enjoy it so much.

Sunday, Nancy and Oscar took me to Bess and Bill's home for tea (they have a wonderful place) and we sat in front of a big fireplace and had a very enjoyable afternoon.

Tonight I am having a little party and have invited about 12 people. Mrs. Kinkead, the woman I am boarding with, has baked a coconut layer cake for me and I'll just serve a buffet supper. Of course I'll have some cocktails and I've rented a radio for the occasion.

Jimmie and Jack have leased an oil station out here and are doing awfully well, and are quite happy to be here. They are busy nights so I don't see much of them. Jimmie has quit drinking and seems to be quite serious about getting down to work so I presume he has at last come to his senses.

With my best regard to you all, I am

As ever,
Valeria

7020 Watseka Ave
Culver City

DEC. 21, 1927

Dear Irma,

Since I have nothing to do, I'm writing to you again. Nothing exciting has happened—in fact, I'm leading a very quiet life and much to my surprise, I like it. I must be getting old! My party at the boys' bungalow went off great—we all had a merry time. All my old friends were there—some of the boys brought liquor, but not enough for anyone to get drunk. I rented a radio for the evening and Mrs. Kinkead baked me a wonderful cake.

As for Christmas, Helen is giving a studio party and I am helping her. We expect the whole Goldwyn organization to call and we have prepared gifts for them all. Of course everybody has contributed to the party so that Helen doesn't have to stand the expense of it. She has the loveliest apartment. We've already bought a tree and decorated it and have holly which we are going to scatter about the place.

We are also having a party at the DeMille studio, but this will take place Saturday afternoon whereas the Goldwyn party will take place in the evening. Sunday I am going to have Christmas dinner at Helen's place and her boy friend will be there too—I'm going to roast a chicken and Helen will make the salad and dessert.

My job here at DeMille's looks very promising. I have been working with those three Yale men on La Rocque's story and it is about finished now. I think they are going to start shooting next week. I worked one evening for Jeanie Macpherson on "The Godless Girl" and last night she sent for me again. I worked until 7:30 and then she asked me if I could work again for her today. In view of this, I am being kept off all other work and being held for Miss Macpherson. So far, she hasn't come in, which accounts for all the leisure time.

I'm just thrilled about it. I never dreamed I'd step into DeMille's, which is such a big studio, and be assigned to such an important person so soon.

The people I am boarding with are lovely to me—it's just like home. I was home one day with a sore throat and Mrs. Kinkead made me stay in bed and made such nice soups and brought them to me in bed and she just looked after me as if I were one of her own. Her home is very pretty too, which perhaps accounts for my liking to stay home evenings. She has a big fireplace in the sitting room and every evening there's a nice fire burning and I just love to sit in one of the big chairs near the fireplace and read. By the way, I've just finished "I promessi Sposi."

DECEMBER 29, 1927

Dear Irma,

Christmas is over and now I'm all agog for New Year's. It rained all day Sunday, but it wasn't cold. The day before it also rained, but it didn't dampen the holiday spirit. Saturday afternoon we had a little party at the office—one girl brought wine and we all contributed something or other and also had a grab bag—all the girls got off about 3 in the afternoon excepting myself. Miss Macpherson called me and I worked like mad on "The Godless Girl" until 6. After that, I went directly to Helen's party and met the whole Goldwyn crowd—Colman had just been there and left so I didn't see him. Well, I had a little of everything, whisky, gin, wine, brandy, but I ate so much that the liquor didn't effect me in the least. From there, I went home to the Kinkeads and they had their little party until about midnight—Santa Claus came and there was much excitement. Mrs. Kinkead was wonderful to me—She put a little tree in my room and bells all around and they all had gifts for me under the tree. Sunday I cooked the Christmas dinner in Helen's apartment and we invited two boys from the studio to join us. As it rained all day, we just stayed in and listened to the radio. Monday, Nancy and Oscar came for me and took me riding all day and we also made several calls.

I am going to a New Year's party and I am expecting to have an awfully good time. Bess and Bill are giving the party and their parties are usually a wow. New Year's Day I am going with the Kinkeads to Pasadena to see the Rose Tournament.

For the last two days I have been working for Harry Carr who is a columnist on the Los Angeles Times—he ranks with Broun and F.P.A. His secretary is sick and I am substituting (he's story advisor at DeMille's). He has a cute office right over one of the stages—the wood work is black—the window drapes and other touches are crimson with large figures of birds (I think that's what they are—they're so futuristic it's difficult to say whether it's a plant, fish or fowl.) I don't have to work very hard. I've just written a lot of letters myself to nuts who write in to him and want to meet him, etc. or want him to give a speech at some club or other. He's a nice old man and very pleasant—but he has a nervous twitching in his face and he's forever opening and closing his eyes. He's out of the office most of the time and I sit around most of the day reading.

While I haven't heard from you in some time, I presume everything is O.K. Wishing you and your family a Happy New Year, I am

As ever,
Valeria

Dear Irma,

It seems like an awfully long time since I last heard from you and I am worried for fear that you are ill or someone in your family is ill. I sincerely hope nothing is wrong.

Things are very quiet at the studios. Warner Bros. has closed its studio and don't think it will reopen until the spring. United Artists has laid off a lot of people; Metro Goldwyn Mayer has laid off about 200; DeMille has laid off about 100—however while other girls who have been here longer than I have have been dismissed, I have been kept on. Moreover, I now am secretary to one of the production managers. While not a very important position, at least I know that I shall be working for some time and furthermore, it's not very difficult and have much leisure, in fact too much idle time.

Mr. Donaldson is the name of my boss. He is manager for "Hold 'em Yale". It's rather a coincidence that I worked with the writers of this story and now I am with the production manager. Having been on the writing end of the story, I was quite prepared to take over my new job with Mr. Donaldson. Knowing the story makes my work with Mr. Donaldson so much easier. We've had lots of bad luck with the picture—we shot one of the football sequences with Rod La Rocque at the beginning and Rod was hurt. This delayed the taking of other football sequences which had to be shot outdoors and we were compelled to shoot our interiors. While we were compelled to work on our interiors, we had marvelous sunshine for outdoor work. Now that our interiors are done and Rod is ready to work outside again, the weather is not so clear. The picture is scheduled to be finished on February 1st and then Mr. Donaldson will be the manager on "Tenth Avenue" (This was a play on Broadway at the beginning of the last theatrical season).

I am leading a very quiet life and saving as much as I can because I want to go abroad next July. I've decided to go back and sell the bonds I have there. Somehow or other I don't feel at rest having money invested in Italy. Helen Kirk is coming with me and this time I intend to enjoy myself. We intend leaving in July and we'll be back at the end of October.

Just at present I am reading a collection of John Keats's poems and I thought the enclosed was a gem. Don't you think so?

Do write to me and let me know what you are doing.

With love to you all, I am

As ever, Valeria

JANUARY 19, 1928

Dear Irma,

I received your letter and was relieved to hear that nothing had happened to you or your family.

Everything is going along very smoothly with me—however, nothing of interest has developed. I am still with Mr. Donaldson and so far as I can see, it will be best for me to stick here until the industry picks up. However, it's not the job I particularly care for—there's not enough to do and it's rather an irksome job to sit around day after day reading and writing letters. That accounts for all the letters you're getting from me. Anyway, it doesn't seem just right to draw $30 per week for doing practically nothing. The man I work for is quite a chaser and he's always telling me about his blondes. I had to buy and wrap some lovely silk underwear—nightgowns, step-ins, lace stockings, etc. for his latest girl (she's a designer at MGM and is quite clever). He made some rather risqué remarks during the process of wrapping them up, but I must say, outside of this incident, he has behaved himself. I was warned to be awfully careful, but I suppose I haven't enough S.A. to suit him and, furthermore, from the conversation, I have gathered he has a penchant for blondes, so that lets me out. He has a reputation for telling naughty stories and jokes—so far he has only told me one and that one wasn't all that bad. It was as follows: "What does a Scotsman do with his old razor blades?" Answer: "He uses them to shave with."

DeMille is shooting "The Godless Girl" and we have a mob of high school girls and boys today on the lot for the riot scene.*

Companionate Marriages has been a topic for discussion here too—in fact, we are planning to do a picture with this title at the studio. Judge Lindsey lectured or debated this subject with some minister here in Los Angeles in November, and since then, numerous articles have been appearing in Los Angeles pro and con. I haven't read anything about it—somehow or other I'm not interested. I take that back—I did read an article—a review on Judge Lindsey's book "Companionate Marriages" and the reviewer stated that while Judge Lindsey's plan seemed to be a good one, he's neglected one thing and that is, "what about the off spring?" The reviewer said something very amusing, which I don't recall offhand, to the effect that Judge Lindsey evidently overlooked the fact entirely that this old

---

* The Godless Girl (about an atheist who finds both love and God by the final reel) would be DeMille's last silent film and his last filmed at what was now Pathé Studios. In the melodrama's pivotal scene Valeria refers to, high school students attack members of "the Godless Society" and a girl is killed in the riot that ensues.

world was still the same and not a Utopian world and therefore there was a risk of children still being born. And this being the case, Judge Lindsey ought to have made some plans for them in his book, whereas he entirely over looked this phase of the situation.

The people I board with are still very nice to me. Tonight I am having my bridge party and Mrs. Kinkead is making a date pudding for dessert to serve my guests. She is also letting me use her big living room and letting me have three bridge tables and the embroidered covers she has for them, as well as tea clothes, etc. I am so satisfied to live here with them and feel perfectly at home. Mrs. Kinkead washes and irons all my things so that I have absolutely nothing to do when I get home evenings but sit down and eat and then I am through. Usually I sit around and read the paper and talk with the family until ten and then I go to bed.

Helen, Elsie and I (we live on the same block in Culver City and just three or four houses apart) are going to study French so that when Helen and I go to Paris (where we intend to stay about 3 weeks) we'll know something. Elsie knows French pretty well which is the reason for her being included, although she is not going abroad. I'm all enthused about my trip and after this trip, I'll be through as far as Europe is concerned. Then my next trip will be to the Hawaiian Islands—I hope you will be in a position to go with me.

Irma, I don't know what's troubling me, but my ideas for a career are just blown up. My ambitions are all changed—what I want now more than anything else is to have a little cottage near Pasadena, a car of my own so that I can go visiting, play golf, tennis, have time to read and perhaps take music lessons or take up some course and be able to entertain my friends without being up to my neck in work and having to just squeeze in my pleasures. Of course, I'll need a husband for this purpose and if Tony comes out here in the spring, I think I'll marry him. He'll have enough money with him to put a down payment of the cottage above referred to and with my own money I shall travel about. Of course I'm assuming that I shall be able to travel say 3 months in a year after I am married. What do you think of this? Would you do likewise? After I am married, with my present connections at the DeMille studio, I think that if I want to work say for 3 or 4 months that I will be able to do so, thereby keeping up with current matters and not losing contacts. Anyway, I'm looking forward to these plans and hope they will materialize. I am also looking forward to the day when you will be out here as my guest. I can just imagine all the things we shall do together. We'll go driving every day, spend a few days at Catalina and just relax.

Very often I think of the days I lived in West New York and worked in New York. How my mother and I just suffered that awful climate and even though it was within our means to make a change, we just stayed because we didn't have the courage of making a change. All those years, just thrown away, when we both could have been out here and happy. I suppose it was fate that kept us there, but I have resolved that if ever things are not just what I want them, I'm going to make a change, even if it's for the worse. We always make changes for the better, at least we hope that, but if not, well, "pacienza" (I'm trying to write "patience" in Italian). If we stay put, we might miss out on something—whereas through change, we may arrive a something or other that will make our lives happier and more complete. Sometimes we encounter new friends who make us happier in knowing them and sometimes we meet people whose lives are such that it is good to know them in order to avoid the things they do, seeing what their mode of living has made of them.

We are having a cold spell now and I'm just about frozen, although the thermometer hasn't registered below 30 in the mornings and evening and rises to about 60 during the day. Somehow or other, after having warm weather for so long, when we get a cold spell, you seem to feel it more.

With kindest regards to all, I am

As ever, Valeria

JANUARY 31, 1928

Dear Irma,

"Hold 'em Yale" company (including Mr. Donaldson) has been away on location for two days and won't return until tomorrow. They are shooting the scene where Rod bests the bandits and he meets the girl and her father who is a Yale professor. It is supposed to be in the Argentine, and while there are any number of country roads where the scenes could have been taken near the studio, the director found that the only road which to his mind resembled an Argentine one was about 121 miles from the studio, near the Mojave desert—that's one reason the picture cost so much.

I told you in my other letters what little work I had to do—well, the situation has been remedied. Two other production managers, Mr. Gurney and Mr. Poppe, have fired their secretaries and now I am working for all three. People are being fired by the hundreds in the studios and things are really in very bad shape. Mr. Gurney is the manager on "The Godless Girl" and Mr. Poppe on "The Cop" and "What Holds Men". William Boyd will play the lead in "The Cop" and I think this picture will be started next week some time. "What

Holds Men" is still in the process of being written and the cast has not yet been selected. Mr. Poppe has just finished "The Skyscraper" with William Boyd and it was previewed last week and is now being titled. I didn't see the preview, but I heard the picture went over big and that Boyd and Alan Hale are very funny and make quite a comedy team. Sue Carol is the leading lady in it.* She is very sweet off stage—just a kid and hasn't been spoiled yet. The hard boiled eggs on this lot are Phyllis Haver and Marie Prevost and they sure are hard—disgustingly so. Lina Basquette who plays the lead in "The Godless Girl" doesn't sound any too refined either—that is she is loud mouthed, but so far I haven't heard anything to her discredit. Of course her late husband, Sam Warner (one of the Warner brothers) died but a few months ago, so perhaps that's what's holding her back.

Did you ever meet Miss Williams who took my job at Langner's? Well, she was married December 22nd and this was a surprise. Ruth, Mr. Schenck's secretary, is also engaged and will be married this summer. I don't see Jimmie and Jack at all—for some reason or other they have dropped me and of course, I'm not pining away, I assure you. They only live about 5 blocks away from me, but they have never troubled themselves to either call me up or drop in to see me. They had been very nice to me in Jersey and did take me to lots of places, but neither one of them were the type that I really would want for friends. It's quite probable that I showed this in my attitude towards them and that's why they have dropped me.

Are you still very busy in the office? I hope you are for I know

---

*Sue Carol left acting in the midthirties and became an agent. In 1939 she "discovered" Alan Ladd, and three years later, she married the soon-to-be star six years her junior; they remained married until his death in 1964.

that means you are making money and I do like to see people prosperous. How is Mary's baby? I can well imagine how happy she must be.

With love to you and your family, I am

As ever,
Valeria

Dear Irma,

It seems like an awfully long time since I've heard from you. I hope you are not ill and it's only because you are busy that you haven't written to me.

I am still at the studio, although my days are numbered. Pathe has bought out DeMille and the whole DeMille crowd is being let out and I presume the Pathe people will bring their own crowd. I am working with Mr. Gurney on "The Godless Girl" and Mr. Poppe on "The Cop" and "Man Made Woman". When these pictures are completed, I expect to be out of a job. However I could have had a very good position, but turned it down. Mr. Sistrom's secretary (Mr. Sistrom is the general manager of the studio and considered a very big man in the industry) intends to leave and she asked me if I would take the job.* It would pay $50 per week and of course there would be no chance of my being let out no matter what happened

*Bill Sistrom did stay with Pathé, even after DeMille negotiated his own exit with Pathé's new "special advisor," Joseph P. Kennedy. Three days after this letter, *Variety* reported, Kennedy was ordering all production departments to discharge their employees on completion of their current productions.

to the studio. She had me work for him two or three nights to see if he would like me (of course I didn't know this at the time. I thought I was merely helping her out) and it seems that he liked the way I took hold of things. The third night I worked, she put the matter up to me and of course I told her that I really couldn't take the job because I didn't expect to work very much longer and I didn't think it would be fair for me to take an important position under such circumstances. I suppose I'll regret not having taken it when the studio closes and I'm out of a job, but just now I don't feel equal to taking an important position. I've gotten into the habit of taking things easy and I just hate to buckle down to something that will require lots of thinking. I'd rather earn $30 and be free than $50 and be constantly worried.

Well, I've gone ahead and bought myself a house in Hollywood. It's stucco (Spanish style) and is on a big lot 50 by 155. You can see the Hollywood hills from the living room windows and while it's outside of the city limits, it only takes 15 minutes to get to Hollywood Boulevard. From the outside the place looks like a private house, but it's a duplex. There are 6 rooms and bath on each side of the house, with all the latest improvement. The house is new (finished 2 months ago). One side is already leased for a year at $65 a month and the other side I am leasing for a year to Nancy and Oscar. There are 3 stucco garages in the back—the lawns and shrubbery are all laid out and planted. There is also a new system of heating installed (separate installation for each side) whereby the turning on and off the gas furnace is electrically controlled, with push buttons in each room. Everything is lovely inside. My plan is that if I marry in the Spring, we can live at the Kinkead's until next Spring when the lease on the one side expires and by that time we shall have enough money to buy all the furniture necessary for such a place. If you come out to visit me next year, I shall have an extra bedroom ready for you. I am really thrilled about the place and while I have put myself into considerable debt, I feel that in time I shall really make quite a bit off the property. Anyway, my rents pay the interest on the mortgages and I have something left over, so I really don't see that I will lose anything.

Since the place is new, there will be no expense for decorating and repairs for some time to come. The rooms are all very prettily decorated and very artistic. The living room fixtures are wrought iron and the Spanish motif predominates throughout so that it will lend itself easily to furnishing. I paid $13,500 for the place and paid $4,000 cash so you see that I have a big mortgage on the place. However the rents more than pay for the interest and the taxes so there should be no difficulty in meeting the payments. Also each tenant pays for its own water, gas and electric and since there are no coal bills, there really won't be many bills to meet.

Saturday night I heard "Aida" with some friends. Rosa Raisa and Charles Marshall sang the leads. It was the Chicago Opera Company who are in Los Angeles for a week. We all enjoyed it very much, especially myself, as I haven't been to any form of entertainment for so long. I've read a few books lately: "Possession" by Louis Bromfield; "The Blood of the Conquerors" by Fergusson and "Vestal Fire" by Compton Mackenzie. The last mentioned book is rather risqué and quite a number of passages in it were embarrassing in its frankness.

I have been feeling uncommonly well the last two weeks and for the first time I am entirely free of a cold. I don't know how long this will last, but I am enjoying my good health.

Give my kindest regards to your family, and hoping to hear from you soon, I am

As ever,
Valeria

P.S. Have you seen Mr. Langner's new play? I understand that it offends these so-called emancipated women and that consequently it is not enjoying the popularity it should.

MARCH 30, 1928
Dearest Irma,

Received your most interesting letter. Also received the various clippings enclosed with your letter.

Last Saturday I was laid off for two or three weeks and was looking forward to doing so many things. I spent Sunday, Monday, Tuesday and Wednesday with Nancy. She has just moved into my house and I thought I'd go over and help her. I also shopped for some plants and bought a bougainvillea. Do you remember how beautiful we thought this vine was when we first saw it in Los Angeles? I never forgot the impression those vivid purple flowers gave me and vowed if I ever got a home of my own I would have this vine growing somewhere near it. Therefore, I bought it and planted it near the garage so that in a few years the whole garage will be covered. Also planted some sweet peas, hollyhocks and some other flowers. Nancy has bought all new furniture for her place and it is so pretty. She made her own window draperies and I helped to line them—we did it all by hand and they look quite artistic. She also has some very vivid hand painted table lamp shades. The whole living room is very colorful and cheerful. I can just imagine how thrilled I will be when I furnish my own place. In fact, I have decided not to go abroad—I think I'd rather put that money into something else—silverware and linen for instance. Yesterday I had planned on going downtown but I was called to help Miss Macpherson at the studio and also had to come in today.

Tony hasn't sold his property yet but hopes to very soon. I believe he has decided to drive out because if he sells his car he will get very little for it and when he arrives in Los Angeles he will have to spend quite a good deal to get a car as good as the one he has. Nancy's husband has promised to take him into the concern he is with in which case he will have an opportunity to work himself up to a very good position. I surely am looking forward to Tony coming out here and being married. I really do care for him and I know that he loves me, so that we ought to be happy.

Jimmie came over to see me yesterday and told me they had sold their gas station and made a profit of $1700. He was awfully thrilled over it—to think that he could make this much in less than 4 months time. They are now going to buy another place and hope to make as much if not more in the same space of time.

It's unfortunate that you and Isabel are not on friendly terms—I can imagine how trying it must be for you. You, Isabel and your mother could be so happy, but as it is, if Isabel's disposition is as you say it would be impossible for any of you to be really happy. Let's hope she will come to her senses and realize the folly of letting a mere man warp her mind and give her a pessimistic outlook on life. I know that I would feel terrible if Tony ever threw me over—but I think if he did, I wouldn't let that ruin my life. Perhaps if Isabel tried getting away from everybody and going to an entirely strange place to live for a while, perhaps she would be able to get out of her present mood. I think if she did this, it wouldn't take her long to realize that home is after all the only place and it would make her appreciate her family more.

Give my regards to your family, and with my best to you,

I remain your friend, Valeria

The address of my new house is 438–440 Alta Vista Blvd. Hollywood. Isn't that pretty? As I told you in my previous letter—you can see the Hollywood hills from the living room windows—hence the name Alta Vista.

JULY 3, 1928
Dear Irma,

Just received your letter and I was sorry to hear of all the illnesses in the family and hope everybody is back to normal by now.

I've had quite a siege myself. As I told you, I was working at an Academy and, on account of the stables being located nearby, I noticed that from the first day I worked there that I had spells of Hay Fever everyday. However, I thought I could work it off, but instead it got worse every day until I had quite a bad attack of asthma and was laid up in bed for over a week. Mrs. Kinkead was awfully good to me and just looked after me day and night. After I was able to get on my feet I went to Lancaster in the Mojave desert to see if I couldn't recuperate more quickly but only stayed 3 days because it was much too dusty for me and I didn't think that dust would help me any. So I packed up and came back home and while I'm not as well as I'd like to be, I'm much better. I've lost about 5 pounds and I'm not at all strong, but I think in another week I'll be O.K.

Monday I dropped in at DeMille's to see one of the girls and I was put to work immediately. One of the writers needed a girl and I was sent to him. He is Leonard Praskin and is writing a story which I think will be called "The Leathernecks" about the United States Marines. I don't know just how long it will last, but I wouldn't mind it lasting for some time. Mr. Praskin is quite interesting and he does speak English beautifully. By the way, he's an Englishman and he does remind me so much of Lawrence Langner. Just at the present moment only one picture is being shot, which is "Show Folks" with Lina Basquette. I was on the set today for some time watching them shoot, but somehow I'm not very enthused about the story.

It surely would be splendid if you got the opportunity to have a dress and hat shop. There is no question as to your making a success of it because I really think your talents lie in that direction. As you say, you would get a great deal of pleasure out of it because you would be doing something that you liked and wanted to do.

It sounds like you are going to have a very enjoyable vacation. I note that after this vacation you are going to save your money and spend your next vacation in California. I shall be looking forward to your coming and staying with me. It will seem awfully good to have you to talk with and revisit the various places of interest with you again. I hope I'll have a car of my own when you come so that we can go about comfortably.

As for Tony—he's having an awfully hard time settling his affairs so that he can leave. His brother was recently run over by an automobile and is now in the hospital with 3 bones broken in his foot so I suppose until he's out, Tony won't be able to leave. He really has so much responsibility for a fellow so young and he's not the type to shirk so it means that until his family is taken care of, he won't leave them. However, I would rather he did his duty and did not leave until he feels he can because then he would have regrets later and perhaps blame me for any qualms of his conscience.

JULY 5, 1928

Yesterday being the 4th, we had a holiday and the Kinkead's asked me to go with them to a picnic. We went to Westlake Park and ate our lunch under one of the big trees overlooking the lake and then I rowed a little. It was a typical family picnic so there was nothing exciting about it. In the evening we fired off some fireworks and then to bed. I've been at the studio all morning but Mr. Praskin hasn't come in yet. I understand that one of his plays has been produced or is going to be produced called "The Charlatan." Have you read anything about it in the dramatic news of the New York papers?

JULY 6, 1928

This is my last day at the studio. I haven't done a thing all day and Mr. Praskin is leaving tomorrow. I've just finished reading Richard Halliburton's "The Royal Road to Romance" which I found very interesting. However, it's given me the wanderlust and I'm fighting a bitter fight to keep myself from going someplace.

Write to me soon again and with love to you, I am

As ever,
Valeria

JULY 19, 1928

Dear Irma,

As I have some spare time, I'm writing to you. I don't know whether I've told you, but Tony has finally succeeded in selling his house and is leaving for California the 29th of this month. As he will drive across the country I suppose he won't reach the coast until about the middle of August. I feel quite elated and I'm positively thrilled at the thought of "roughing" it in Yosemite on our honeymoon. I don't know just how long we'll be away, but I imagine it will be about 3 weeks.

This week I am working for Mr. MacMahon who is writing a novel of "The Godless Girl."* Mr. MacMahon is a loveable old man and I enjoy working for him. However, I think he will be through this week so I'll have to look about for something else. Over a week ago, I worked two days for a writer in Hollywood in his apartment. He was an Englishman and it was rather thrilling. We made coffee and he served it to me and all in all felt quite at home, although when I first entered I did wonder if he was O.K. However, he was in every way a gentleman and an interesting one at that. He dictated the whole story to me and I brought it home to type (Mr. Kinkead has a machine at home) and Mr. Spencer (the writer) called for it at my home. We spent a delightful afternoon talking about various things and he told me he would have me again when he tackled his next story.

Last week I wasn't working so spent most of my time with a Mrs.

---

* "Novelizing" popular movies was a common practice. Grosset and Dunlap were the primary publishers of books "from Photoplays," which were laced with photographs from the movie and were often written by someone who had nothing to do with the making of the film.

Neff whom I met through Mrs. Kinkead. She is a domestic science teacher and has a very charming son and a lovely English type home. She asked me to spend several days with her which I did and we had a jolly time together. She drove me in her car to the beach almost every day and one evening she and her son took me to a show. Next week, if I'm not working, we've planned to play golf together.

We are making three pictures on the lot now. "Singapore Sal" with Phyllis Haver; "Marked Money" with Junior Coghlan, George Duryea, Virginia Bradford and Tom Kennedy and "Show Folks" with Lina Basquette. I go on the sets almost every day and watch for a while, but I don't get the thrill out of the game as I used to.

I am anxious to hear from you as to whether you are going ahead with the proposition you mentioned in your last letter, that is the dress and millinery shop. I'm hoping you'll go into it and make such a success of it that you'll have to have a Hollywood branch and perhaps you may manage the Hollywood shop. How about it?

We are now beginning to have some warm weather—it was so cool the whole month of June that I felt uncomfortable.

I've been buying a few things in preparation for my honeymoon, but nothing very much. I'll wait until after I'm married, then I will be able to know just how much I will want to spend and know, perhaps, what I really want. I figure it would be rather foolish to buy a lot of finery now when I expect to be "roughing" it on my honeymoon.

Hoping you are well and with love to you all,

I am,
As ever,
Valeria

Dear Irma,

Received your letter and am glad to hear you are all well. I am feeling much better too.

For the last three weeks I have been working for Mr. MacMahon who is writing a novel based on DeMille's picture "The Godless Girl." I surely enjoy doing this work and I'll be sorry when I'm finished. Mr. MacMahon writes about three chapters a day. He usually dictates to me directly on the machine. I write just a rough draft—he corrects and revises and then I type it on good paper. We've already completed half the novel and sent it to the publishers in New York. We are using stills from the picture for illustrations in the book and it was quite a job typing the captions for each picture on a slip of paper and pasting it on the back of the picture for the publisher's guidance. In order to follow the picture more or less faithfully, Mr. MacMahon takes me into the projection room where the picture is run and he then dictates notes to me. This is about the hardest part of the job because he dictates the action of each scene as it unfolds and as there is much action in each scene, he must dictate very quickly in order to let nothing escape. However, he is a very kind old man and he hasn't said anything at all where I have to leave spaces because he dictated too fast and I couldn't get it.

Tony hasn't left yet and I'm wondering if he'll ever come. This waiting business is beginning to get on my nerves and if he doesn't come soon, I think I'll write him not to come at all.

Did you know Norma Talmadge and her husband Joseph Schenck

are no longer living together? I believe they are going to be divorced very shortly—this is merely a rumor. Of course Norma has been carrying on dreadfully with Roland Gilbert for the last year and she hasn't taken any pains to conceal from the public how she felt towards him. And so it goes—all marriages seem to break sooner or later amongst the movie people.

The "talkies" is creating quite a revolutionizing effect in the industry and productions are being held up pending the formation of new policies taking this new element into consideration. I don't know what it will lead to, but things are changing and it seems to me that speaking pictures will be all the go in the future. Dramatic schools are flourishing all over and stars are beginning to really cultivate their voices. MGM is building two sound stages (noise proof) for the making of such pictures and I suppose other studios are doing likewise.

I hope you have a pleasant trip and you must send me some pictures of the place as well as of yourself. With love to you, I am

As ever,
Valeria

....

The "talkies" did indeed revolutionize the industry. *The Jazz Singer,* released in the fall of 1927, was initially greeted by many in the business as a novelty. No less an authority than Thomas Edison, who had experimented with synchronizing sound with film as early as the 1890s, never believed there was much future in it. Although always confident that "voices can be reproduced to fit in just the right place" on the screen, in 1927 Edison told *Film Daily* he considered sound pictures "a waste of time. I don't think the talking picture will ever be successful in the United States. Americans prefer silent drama . . . they will never get enthusiastic over any voices being mingled in."

For months, studio heads took comfort in such remarks, in part because to believe otherwise meant a total change in the way they produced their films. As Cecil B. DeMille summed up their collective dilemma, "To bring in sound meant huge new expenditures, both in the studios and in the theaters and the scrapping of much of the existing studio equipment. All this would be enormous waste if, after the novelty wore off, the public preferred their screens to be silent."

As Valeria notes, this decision not to act but rather to wait and see what others would do resulted in many studios being nearly idle for the first half of 1928. Then, as the box office success of "talkies" could not be argued with, the rush began to add sound to as many films and theaters as possible as quickly as possible.

The Godless Girl was made as a silent film and released that way in August 1928. Then, after DeMille left the studio, a sound segment was filmed, and music and sound effects were added for release the following year. For more than a year, many films had partial sound, perhaps only music or sound effects and a scene or two with dialogue. And of course theaters had to be wired for the sound to be heard, and that process also took several years to accomplish. MGM's biggest star, Greta Garbo, wouldn't release her first sound film, *Anna Christie*, until 1930.

Valeria had a front-row seat to the dramatic changes taking place in the film business, and she seems to have taken them as they came. She was also obviously aware of the tenuous nature of her position at the studio and that made the idea of marriage all the more attractive.

All her other friends were married or getting married, and "love" rarely entered into the equation. Most of her friends had married the man who had finally asked them. As Valeria said about Nancy and Flo, "they are both grabbing at the chance even though both the fellows in question are not quite what they expected to marry." Valeria did exactly the same, for she certainly hadn't pined for Tony after she returned to California and left him in the East. She never mentions the fact that he was six years her junior as a concern. She took solace in Tony's adoration and assured herself she would learn to love him, or at least all the things he did for her, as she vacillated between ennui and excitement.

AUGUST 7, 1928

Dear Irma,

Thank you so much for your good wishes, Irma, and I shall be sure to wear the four leaf clover in my shoe on my wedding day—and if it brings me luck, you'll have all my blessings (if that means anything) for the rest of your life.

(Aug. 9) Monday I received a wire from Tony from Clinton, Iowa so that I'm expecting to get a wire from him in about five days to meet him in Sacramento where we will be married. Last night Mrs. Kinkead gave a lovely dinner for my friends and announced my engagement and it was all quite thrilling. She is also making me a lovely white satin nightgown and a pink satin negligee trimmed with cream silk lace. I really think she is more excited than I am about it. Somehow or other I just can't seem to get terribly excited over the prospect of being married. While I was thrilled with the dinner (she had flowers, yellow and orchid, all over the dining room and living room, next door to us is a nursery and we are quite friendly so they supplied us with all the flowers—then she had yellow and

194

orchid candles and everything else was carried out in these colorings) I missed all my old friends. How I wished that you had been there.

I have finished working for Mr. MacMahon on the novel and am now working for Tay Garnett on the script of "The Spieler."[*] He is rushing me quite hard on this story—dictated from 10 in the morning until 4 in the afternoon and I had only half the next day to transcribe my notes. The story is a very exciting one about Carnival life and therefore I don't mind the hard work attached to it. I think it will keep me busy all week and after that I am hoping to leave for Sacramento.

I was delighted to hear about your meeting the man from Minneapolis and I'm hoping that some day you will be living there and in this way be able to visit me occasionally in California and perhaps I can visit you too. Won't this be nice? Perhaps you might be able to get him to come to California to live. (I'm assuming of course that my wish will come true and you will be married too)

As for a wedding present, really anything you want to give me will be appreciated. You know I have very little of anything and I know that whatever you may send me will suit me, because I know your taste is always good.

AUGUST 30, 1928

Dear Irma,

I wrote the enclosed letter but never mailed it. Since then many things have happened. First of all Tony arrived in Culver City Sun-

---

[*] *The Spieler* was released in December in both a silent version and one with sound sequences, only four months after Valeria worked on the script.

day morning, August 12. Monday we went to Los Angeles and got our license. Monday night, without any previous symptoms, I got a severe attack of asthma. Tuesday morning I asked Mrs. Kinkead to go with me to Long Beach where there is a man who is performing wonders in healing. I decided it would be best to get away right away so Tony carried me into his car and they propped me up comfortably with pillows and away we went. Mrs. Kinkead came along and on arriving at Long Beach, she hunted for a furnished apartment and we were duly installed. Mrs. Kinkead's mother who also has asthma is down here taking treatments and when she saw how bad I was she gave me some Chinese pills to take. I took 2 of them and was relieved and by Friday the 17th I had no trace of asthma.

Tony, Mrs. Kinkead and I lived together those few days and on the 17th we all went back to Culver City where I was married in the home of a friend who happens to be a judge and he married us. Saturday morning Tony and I left for Catalina and we stayed only until the next day. We came right back to our Long Beach apartment and we've been spending our honeymoon here because I was not really strong enough to travel. The doctor who is treating me says that I ought to get well in 2 to 3 months time, but I shall always have to be careful because my lungs are weak and I have little resistance. However the week I've been here has done me a world of good. Perhaps it's because I'm so happy with Tony. He has been so good and considerate and patient. He is now working for an insurance company here in Long Beach and I think things will brighten up now that I am feeling better. The days I was sick Tony waited on me and did all the work and was as handy around the house as a woman which was quite a surprise to me.

I received your card from Jamaica and I'm anxious to hear from you regarding your trip.

With all my love, I am

As ever,
Valeria

Mrs. Baragona
1819 E. 4th St.
Long Beach, California

SEPTEMBER 23, 1928

Dear Irma,

Well, I am back again from Long Beach and am now domiciled in Hollywood. We've rented the cutest little furnished apartment about a block away from my house. Tony started looking for work this week and he was supposed to start to work with a real estate concern today, but I'm not sure whether he will take the job or wait for something better to turn up. As for myself, I've worked all week at the Pathe studio and will work this week too. Just now I'm the steno in charge of what we call "Sound Unit #1". It's the first talkie we are making and everything is more or less experimental. The picture is "Gang War" with Olive Borden and Jack Pickford. I also worked a day for William Cowen who is a new director and just completed "Ned McCobb's Daughter" which, according to the magazines of the industry, is a very good picture. Also did more work on the novel of "The Godless Girl" and worked on a story called "Geraldine" with Marion Nixon and Eddie Quillan.

My health is much better, although I sure did have a tough time of it. While I was in Long Beach we went to Laguna Beach with some friends of mine to spend the weekend at their cabin and during the night I was taken sick with asthma so we left the next day. The attack only lasted about 5 hours. Then about a week later we visited the Kinkeads in Culver City and we planned to stay over night. I had been in bed only about 2 hours when I got another attack and 2:30 I was so choked up I thought I was dying. I woke Tony up and told him to get out the car and take me out to the car and we drove back. By the time I reached Long Beach (about 4 in the morning) I was better again and I feel very well, so it must be that there is something or other in certain places which gives me my attacks and hereafter when I feel an attack coming on, I'll just drive to another place.

Nancy gave me a shower last week and Mrs. Kinkead gave me one Saturday night so that I received some very pretty gifts and Tony got to meet all my friends. They have all accepted him and they all like him, which makes me very happy. I took Tony over to the United Artists studios and showed him around and he was so thrilled when he saw Doug Fairbanks, Camilla Horn, Lupe Velez and John Barrymore and we watched them shooting Doug's next picture for a long time.

My address is now 522 N. Alta Vista Blvd. Hollywood. I'd like to hear from you and about your trip. By the way, Tony and I visited Tia Juana, but it doesn't look half as wicked as when we were there together. After the town burnt down about two years ago it was rebuilt with substantial brick and stucco buildings and the streets are wide and paved, so that outside of there being a saloon in every building, it looks just like any other California town. We also visited the caves of La Jolla. That sure is a beautiful spot. We sat on the rocks and watched the waves dashing against them for about an hour. The ocean looked so blue and the sky didn't have a cloud in it.

Dear Irma, I'm so happy with Tony. The more I'm with him, the more I love him. He was so patient and good when I was sick and he is affectionate and kind to me—it just seems too good to last. I'm always afraid that something will happen, because I somehow feel that one cannot enjoy lasting happiness on earth. I guess it's silly to feel this way, but you no doubt know just what I'm driving at.

With love to you, your mother and Isabel, I am

As ever,
Valeria

DECEMBER 15, 1928

Dear Irma,

Just a line while I have nothing to do. We have been so busy at the studio that I hardly know how to conduct myself today now that things have slowed up. We have been inserting dialogue in all our pictures that is: "Show Folks"—"Sal of Singapore"—"Gang War"—"Geraldine"—"Love in the Desert"—"Shady Lady"—"The Spoiler"—"Blockade"—"The Godless Girl"—"The Jazz Age"—"Leathernecks"—"Noisy Neighbors"—"Office Scandal"—"Square Shoulders"—and we have just finished our 100% talkie "The Missing Man" and still working on the script of "Listen Baby" so you see that there's been a lot to do.

I had to go into the projection room on "Love in the Desert" and the dialogue sounded very good, but from my standpoint, it was not so good because I had to take down every word spoken by the various characters and at times three people almost spoke simultaneously. I had to have the reel run about 6 times before I could get all the dialogue correct. Scott Darling finished the script of "Listen Baby" but Casey Robinson who is going to direct it has rewritten the whole thing and unless they decide that his version is O.K., I guess we'll be rewriting it again.

"Leathernecks" was previewed a few nights ago and from what I hear, it's going to be a good picture and may be classed a "road show" picture. However, most of our pictures are ordinary program pictures so I guess you rarely see any of them.

I am at present working in the production end of the studio and at times I am called up to take charge of the stenographic department. In fact, all the men on the lot who want work done have to call me and I had to hire and fire girls according to our needs about a week ago. However, this was only while the head of the department was sick and I ran things while she was out. Anyway, it makes me feel good to know that they have enough confidence in me to let me run things in case of an emergency. In view of my present job, I have to stay at my desk all day and am not sent out to writers any more. Of course I'd rather be sent out to writers, but for the time being I have to take charge of the production office until the girl who had charge of it comes back which will not be for another month yet.

We are planning to have a big Christmas party at the studio this year and Tony is terribly worried for fear that I'll drink too much and perhaps disgrace myself. Of course I've promised to behave myself but he doesn't like the idea very much. He wouldn't mind if he could be present. Knowing that we'll have wine, etc., he's afraid some of the men might take advantage of me. You know what bad reputations studio men have! Tony is still very much interested in his studies. He's given up his job at the theatre because one of the men in the clinic is getting Tony in the night clinic where he can gain much practical experience thereby helping him get through more quickly.

I had one of those stores send you a box of dates, figs, etc. a few days ago and you ought to get it in the next ten days. If you don't, please let know so that I can get them to make good on the shipment by sending another box.

With love to you and your family, I am

As ever,
Valeria

JANUARY 19, 1929

Dear Irma,

It does seem so long since I've heard from you. I hope everything is O.K.

Everything is very slow here at the studio. In fact, no picture is in production at the present time and nearly everyone has been laid off temporarily. There are only 3 girls in the stenographic department and we've been kept busy because Casey Robinson has written and rewritten "Listen Baby" about a half dozen times. However, they've postponed the making of this picture at the present time so that we won't even have this to fall back on.

Tony still goes to school and he is so interested in his studies that he is taking up extra work at night.* Also the head of the clinic has taken a liking to Tony and allows him to go in the public clinic three nights a week. Of course all he does is observe, but he's glad of this

---

*Tony was studying chiropractic medicine.

chance because all the other fellows have to put in at least one year of school before they are allowed to observe in the clinic. The students give affairs about once a month and last month Tony put on a little comedy sketch which I helped him write and it went over so big that he's been delegated to put on another sketch for the next affair. We have a lot of fun doing this and it also helps Tony to get a firm foothold with the heads of the school.

Last week I was off for a few days with the flu, but I've recovered fully and now feel very well again. One day when I was home, Tony and I went up to the mountains and spent the afternoon outdoors in the sun. It was lovely and warm and the country looked beautiful. All the orange trees are loaded with golden oranges and we stopped near a little lake that was surrounded with calla lilies in bloom. It did look so pretty. I had put up some lunch so we parked near the lake and got out. There was a rustic bench with a roof of palm trees over it and we sat there and ate our lunch.

Gloria Swanson is making a picture on our lot called "Queen Kelly" with Von Stroheim directing. I have only seen Gloria once. She seems quite friendly and I was surprised to see that her hair wasn't dark. It's quite a light brown. Somehow or other I had the idea she was very dark.

I have the cutest little gray cat here near my machine. He hardly lets me work—he's just jumping all over trying to catch my carriage. He sits here nearly all day either sleeping or playing. Now he's all curled up in my filing basket.

No doubt you read about Frances Marion's husband dying.[*]

---

[*]Frances Marion's husband, the cowboy star Fred Thomson, died of tetanus on Christmas Day 1928 at the age of thirty-eight. He was the idol of young boys, headlines throughout the country mourned his death, and the throngs outside his funeral were said to rival Valentino's.

That surely was a shock to everyone. I feel so sorry for Miss Marion because I know how fond she was of him. I guess we're not supposed to have everything on this earth. Sometimes when Tony and I are together, I begin to fear that something might happen to blight our happiness. Tony is so good to me. He just can't seem to do too much for me and there's one thing that I do enjoy and that is having my cup of black coffee in bed in the morning. When my mother was alive, she used to bring it to me and of course when she couldn't, I'd bring it to her. Of course, after she died, no one brought me coffee in bed and now after all these years, I have someone who is reviving the old habit—and how I love it!

Write me soon and with love to you and your family, I am

As ever,
Valeria

MAY 10, 1929

Dear Irma:

What has happened to you? Have you been ill—or someone in your family? I'm really worried because I haven't heard from you in months. I have been waiting and waiting for a reply to my letter, but since I didn't get one, I decided to write again in order to relieve my state of mind. I sincerely hope nothing is wrong and that you have only been negligent.

We have been awfully busy here at the studio making talkies. Ina Claire is making a picture here called "The Awful Truth." This is a play by Arthur Richman and he is on the lot adapting the play to the screen. I suppose you heard the news about Ina and John

Gilbert.* It surely did surprise us all on the lot. We are also making an all talkie with Ann Harding called "Paris Bound" and a college story with Sally O'Neil and Eddie Quillan. We are also casting for four operas we are going to make and about 20 other pictures, so you can imagine how busy we are. Things are quite interesting with the talkies now, and we do hear marvelous music—instrumental and vocal now that we are having so many coming to the studio for voice tests, etc. I am no longer working for writers but am now assistant supervisor in the stenographic dept. and have been given a $5 dollar raise—so I feel quite elated and of course I can do more as I please now and not have to work so hard. Tony is getting along very well in school and he is now in a private clinic so that he receives a dollar for each patient he treats. We are both so happy—and I have been feeling so well that I almost feel as if I were sitting on top of the world.

Do write to me soon and let me know what you are doing and how you are.

*With love to you,
I am, As Ever,
Valeria*

* Ina Claire and Jack Gilbert's marriage surprised the film colony in 1929 because he was assumed to be still in love with Garbo. Gilbert's marriage to Claire was his third, and they divorced two years later.

EPILOGUE

The Pathé studio where Valeria was working was sold to RKO in late 1930 and then several years later to David Selznick. It would change hands several more times (Sony sold it again in 2005), yet the mansion—office building and much of the lot remain as they were when Valeria was there.

Sam Goldwyn continued as a successful independent producer, switching to sound films with one of his biggest successes, *Bulldog Drummond*, starring Ronald Colman. (Unlike his former co-star, Vilma Banky, who retired with the coming of talkies, the stage-trained Colman flawlessly made the transition to speaking roles.) Goldwyn worked with many of Hollywood's greatest talents, and in 1947, he finally won the Academy Award for Best Picture with *The Best Years of Our Lives*, written by Robert Sherwood, directed by William Wyler, and photographed by Gregg Toland, with an all-star cast headed by Myrna Loy and Fredric March.

Frances Goldwyn remained devoted to her husband for the rest of their lives; Sam died at the age of ninety-four in 1974 and Frances, twenty years younger, died in early 1976. As Sam Junior recalled, "My mother's life was over after Dad died." Frances was buried next to her husband in the family crypt at Forest Lawn, but she had long before made arrangements for her dearest friend, the man she called "the only person I ever truly loved," George Cukor, to be buried there as well, as indeed he was after his death in 1983.

Without necessarily realizing it, Valeria had witnessed a major shift in the business of filmmaking. During its first few decades, the doors were wide open to women and they flourished, not just as actresses, but as directors and writers. Lois Weber, Cleo Madison, Gene Gauntier, and dozens of other women were successful and prolific directors. Before 1925, almost half of all films were written by women. Yet as banks and Wall Street began to invest and studios became major economic forces, the work became more respectable and better paid; men wanted the jobs. Some of the early pioneers, particularly writers such as Frances Marion, Anita Loos, and Jeanie Macpherson and the editors Margaret Booth, Blanche Sewall, and Anne Bauchens continued to be in demand, but by 1930, they were the exception and no longer the rule.

While she worked in Hollywood, Valeria had her share of role models and occasionally exhibited signs of real ambition. At various points she expressed hopes of becoming a script girl or a screenwriter. She was "thrilled" when Frances Marion took her under her wing, but while Valeria took advantage of other opportunities when they presented themselves, perhaps she was too intimidated to follow through on Frances's offers. It seems that Valeria was never passionate enough about changing course to exercise the persistence it would have required. Marriage was always there, lurking as the other "career choice."

The theme of finding a husband laces through Valeria's letters over the years. Like many of her friends, she looked at almost every man who came into her sphere as a potential husband, to the point that serious friendships with men were not allowed to develop or really enjoyed in the moment. When she made her chart on the pros and cons of marrying her friend Muschi, she found him "charming, talented, fine and interesting," yet she "decided the odds were against him" and dropped him accordingly.

Tony was there waiting on the sidelines and more than willing. He clearly adored her and, if she was only fond of him in return, she assured Irma she did "really care for him." More than being in love with Tony, Valeria was in love with the idea of being married, in love with the fantasy of what she imagined marriage to be. Who the husband was didn't matter as much as the fact that he was the necessary means to attain the lifestyle she envisioned for herself: "a car of my own so that I can go visiting, play golf, tennis, have time to read and perhaps take music lessons or take up some course and be able to entertain my friends without being up to my neck in work and having to just squeeze in my pleasures," and to "travel say 3 months a year." (While she clearly spent quite a bit of time working out the details in her mind, once she entered the reality of married life, she only casually took up hobbies and never traveled extensively again.)

Valeria left Pathé shortly after this last letter in the early summer of 1929 and her son, Tony Jr., was born on January 26, 1930. By 1932, her husband had finished his schooling in Los Angeles, and the family moved to Santa Barbara, where Tony established what would become his successful chiropractic practice with an office at 1427 Anacapa Street.

For several years Valeria worked for local writers typing and editing their manuscripts, but by the mid-1930s she was becoming more and more obsessed with her health. She convinced herself that she couldn't go to other people's homes because they might have a cat or a dog and she couldn't go to dances or parties because she might be subjected to smoke or dust — any of which might spark an onset of asthma. Gradually she became so cautious that she took to her bed. To Valeria, staying in her room day after day was totally rational — it was the only way to stay healthy.

Tony was a doting husband and father while Valeria entertained herself with crossword puzzles, reading the *New Yorker*, and attending the occasional movie or concert. Margery Baragona remembers her father-in-law as being "very maternal" to Valeria. "I don't mean feminine, but he took care of her and was very solicitous, waiting on her and bringing her coffee in bed and anything else she needed." The Baragonas continued to live in their comfortable home at 416 E. Anapamu with a cottage in the back that they rented out. Young Tony was sent to Catholic schools until high school and went to the University of California at Santa Barbara for two years before being called up to serve in Korea in the Naval Reserve. When he returned, he married a friend from high school, Margery Marcus, and they moved to Berkeley, where he finished college at the University of California before beginning a successful career as a creative director for advertising companies.

"Dear Irma" had saved all her letters from Valeria and, in a visit to California in 1951, brought the letters with her and presented them back to Valeria. The two old friends went through them together, laughing and reliving their memories. Irma never married, and while she always lived in the New York area, she traveled frequently.

Valeria stayed friends with Nancy and Flo, who remained in Los Angeles but often visited Santa Barbara alone or together or with their husbands. They too remained married to the men who had asked them, not in particularly satisfying relationships, but it was what they had sought and the deal they had made. Finding a husband had been a goal for so long that after the initial glow of accomplishing it had faded, the women found themselves flailing and then caught in a web of their own (and society's) making.

Valeria told Nancy and Flo that her studio days were her most joyful, back when they had been "bachelor girl friends" happy in their "Adamless Eden." Their continued friendship sustained them, and when Valeria died in 1959, Nancy and Flo lifted her from the coffin to give her a final hug.

Tony Baragona died in 1991, and when Tony Jr., who had also made his home in Santa Barbara, passed away in 2004, he was survived by his wife, Margery, their three sons, Marc, Paul, and Matthew, and six grandchildren.

SUGGESTED READING

The twenties were such a vital time in Hollywood, and a variety of books capture that era in wonderful ways. Carey McWilliams and Kevin Starr are the most authoritative writers on California history, and their books are also eminently readable. Another book that portrays the time and place in a fun, flowing style is *The Incredible Land* by the bon vivant travel writer Basil Woon. (His other works include *When It's Cocktail Time in Cuba*, which gives you an idea of the tone.) And of course it was working on my own book, *Without Lying Down: Frances Marion and the Powerful Women of Early Hollywood*, that I first came in contact with Valeria and her family.

Other books — several of which are out of print but easily available through libraries or used-book sites — I have particularly enjoyed, learned from, and/or quoted from include

Berg, A. Scott. *Goldwyn: A Biography*. New York: Ballantine Books, 1989.

Brownlow, Kevin. *The Parade's Gone By*. New York: Ballantine Books, 1969.

———. *Hollywood: The Pioneers*. New York: Alfred A. Knopf, 1979.

Ellenberger, Allan R. *The Valentino Mystique*. Jefferson, N.C.: MacFarland, 2005.

Fairbanks, Douglas, Jr. *The Salad Days*. New York: Doubleday, 1988.

Guiles, Fred Laurence. *Marion Davies*. New York: McGraw Hill, 1972.

Langner, Lawrence. *The Magic Curtain*. New York: E. P. Dutton, 1951.

Leider, Emily. *Dark Lover: The Life and Death of Rudolph Valentino*. New York: Farrar, Straus and Giroux, 2003.

Loos, Anita. *A Girl Like I*. New York: Viking, 1966.

Marion, Frances. *Off with Their Heads: A Serio-comic Tale of Hollywood*. New York: Macmillan, 1972.

Parrish, Robert. *Growing Up in Hollywood*. New York: Harcourt Brace Jovanovich, 1976.

Schulberg, Budd. *Moving Pictures: Memories of a Hollywood Prince*. New York: Stein and Day, 1981.

Scott, Evelyn F. *Hollywood When Silents Were Golden*. New York: McGraw Hill, 1972.

Selznick, Irene Mayer. *A Private View*. New York: Alfred A. Knopf, 1983.

Thompson, Frank, ed. *Henry King Director*. Based on interviews by David Shepard and Ted Perry. Los Angeles: Directors Guild of America, 1995.

◉

EDITOR'S NOTE

....

Valeria Belletti first came into my life almost eight years ago, just after my book *Without Lying Down: Frances Marion and the Powerful Women of Early Hollywood* was published. I was fortunate to hear from many people I'd never met who were touched by Frances's story, and among them was Margery Baragona. She wrote that after reading my book she realized she was "sitting on history"; her mother-in-law had been Sam Goldwyn's secretary, and in the family cupboards were dozens of letters she had sent to her girlfriend Irma from the studios during the 1920s. It turned out that I had written about Valeria without knowing her name, for both Frances Marion and Hedda Hopper had spoken of Goldwyn's secretary being pivotal in the "discovery" of Gary Cooper. Now Margery confirmed that story and told me new ones.

Margery and her husband, Tony, were in Santa Barbara and I was in Connecticut at the time, so we talked on the phone and I encouraged them to donate the letters to the Margaret Herrick Library of the Academy of Motion Picture Arts and Sciences, where they could be read by researchers. In passing I mentioned the letters to my friend Emily Leider, who was working on a biography of Rudolph Valentino, and didn't think any more about it until I heard from Emily several months later — she was not only thrilled with the letters' contents (the information on Valentino gave her specific dates and locations she would not otherwise have found) but insisted I read them all as soon as possible: "Cari, they stand on their own and are fabulous. You *have* to get them published."

At that moment, the last thing I wanted was a new project. Another friend I had made during the course of writing *Without Lying Down* was Mary Anita Loos, Anita's niece and heir. In the process of our meetings, she brought out boxes and boxes of Anita's unpublished manuscripts. Their contents were too good to pass up, so together Mary Anita and I read through them and they eventually became *Anita Loos Rediscovered: Film Treatments and Fiction by Anita Loos, Creator of "Gentlemen Prefer Blondes."*

Yet knowing Emily was not given to hyperbole, I made time on my next trip to California to visit Tony and Margery and to read all the letters. Like Emily, I was charmed by the style and enamored with the cast of characters and the detailed descriptions of the studio life. I asked my friend Bridget Terry, a writer and producer, to read them, and she confirmed my reaction, adding that with a little fleshing out, the letters could stand alone as a great script, better than "The Lot," "Remember WHEN," or any period program that had been done to date.

Most important, I found that Valeria's words stayed with me. So many of her comments seemed contemporary — the way her spirits rose and fell with weekend box office results and her respect for her bosses' talent even when she ran out of patience with their childish temperament. In contrast, her use of the royal "we" and references to bootleggers were dated, if endearing. And it was more than a little heartbreaking to think of what she and other women like her would have been able to accomplish professionally if more opportunities had been open to them. Although women are more visible in a variety of roles behind the camera today, the fact remains that only 7 percent of the top 200 films of 2005 were directed by women. We have a long way to go before we return to the numbers of women prospering in the business in, say, 1919.

Voices such as Valeria's are rarely if ever heard. Thousands of now-nameless women worked in Hollywood in the twenties as secretaries, playing an important part of the studios' success, yet we know little or nothing about them. They took the work just as seriously as the directors and producers who lace Hollywood histories, yet if women like Frances Marion and Anita Loos, who were making several thousand dollars a week, are sadly missing from most of the histories, how can we expect to find the Valerias, who took home $40 for their six-day work weeks? One volume of letters can hardly balance the scales, but perhaps other letters stashed in other cupboards will be valued and made available — to inspire, clarify, and enhance our understanding of their work, their worlds, and their lives.

Since this book has been years in the making, there are innumerable people who played important roles. First of course is "Dear Irma" Prina herself, who received Valeria's letters and had the foresight to save them and return them to her decades later. And then the Baragonas, who, from the time I broached the possibility of publishing the letters, were supportive in the gracious way I soon learned to expect from them. Over the years their faith and bonhomie never wavered. Even facing death, Tony, with his dry humor, sharp intelligence, and perspective, continued to amaze, and Margery's sense of fun and appreciation of life remain an inspiration.

Charlotte Sheedy, an elegant and always illuminating presence in my life, gave willingly to the project, and Mary Francis and Suzanne Knott of the University of California Press became partners in the enterprise at every turn. Edith Gladstone played a pivotal role. Particular thanks and appreciation go to this book's earliest readers, Emily Leider and Bridget Terry, as well as Mary Lea Bandy, who fell in love with the idea and whose kindness, professionalism, and friendship over the years make a book unto itself. More timely encouragement and assistance came from my beloved Martha Lorah, who devotedly served Frances Marion for decades as her secretary and whose effervescent spirit continues to inspire; my mother, Catherine

Beauchamp, who faithfully reads, copyedits, and raves about everything I write; and Bruce Handy of *Vanity Fair*, who has become a dependable friend in the process of teaching me that the best editor can be an invaluable partner as well as truly elevate the work.

Peter Biskind, Steve Ross, and Marc Wanamaker were particularly generous with their time, support, and direction, while Scott Berg went above and beyond, not only in his willingness to answer questions and go back into his own research but in channeling Irene Selznick and helping me the way she helped him. The enthusiasm and cooperation of both Sam Goldwyn Jr. and Rorri Feinstien were especially meaningful.

As in everything else I have worked on for the past decade plus, Kevin Brownlow metaphorically sat at my shoulder, assuring me while keeping me aiming for the highest standards, both personally and professionally. Letters such as Valeria's are the heir apparent to the oral histories of the Hollywood pioneers that Kevin so lovingly recorded and that are so crucial to historians today. We are unable to follow up with questions to the letters, but they are also unfiltered by any concern for posterity.

Madeline Matz at the Library of Congress and Ned Comstock of the University of Southern California were veritable fountains of information as well as the kindest and most generous of friends. At the Academy of Motion Picture Arts and Sciences, I must thank Randy Habercamp as well as Linda Mehr, Howard Prouty, Barbara Hall, and Jenny Romero of the Margaret Herrick Library.

For their support, suggestions, and general tolerating of my questions and ramblings, I deeply appreciate the focus and friendship of Jimmy Bangley, Terry Christensen, Virginia Dean, Allan Ellenberger, Michelle Fuetsch, Phyllis Guss, Gene Hatcher, Ellen Hume, Karen Johnson, Peter Jones, Fay Kanin,

Julie La'Bassiere, Peter Morgan, Maggie Mosher, Mona Onstead, Maggie Renzi, Susy Smith, Michelle Sullivan, and Marina Zenovich.

My immediate family, Catherine, Tom, Teo, and Jake, know how much I love and depend upon them. I am particularly appreciative of their understanding of the joy I find in my alternative world. Frances, Valeria, and all the wonderful women who have gone before give me such strength and the knowledge that I am just another link in the chain. Hopefully their stories will give other women the same sense of liberation.

INDEX

Academy Award for Best Picture
(1947), Goldwyn, 205
Academy of Motion Picture Arts
and Sciences, Margaret Herrick
Library, 211
Adrian (designer), 130
Agnew, Bobby, 140
Aida, 183
alcohol, 140, 200; bootleggers,
56, 212; at Goldwyn office,
52–53, 104–5; on Hearst's
yacht, 89; Italy, 151; Prohibition,
56–57, 89
*Anita Loos Rediscovered: Film Treat-
ments and Fiction by Anita Loos,
Creator of "Gentlemen Prefer
Blondes"* (Beauchamp), 212
Anna Christie, 193
Ann's an Idiot, 17–18, 24
Arlen, Michael, 99
Arnold Waterlow (Sinclair), 46
Artland Club, 134–35
Astor, Mary, 140
The Awful Truth, 203

Banky, Vilma, 34, 35, 39–40,
66–67, 161; *The Dark Angel*,
40, 49, 57, 66, 79; fan photos,

79, 102; Goldwyn-Howard marriage dinner, 35; marriage, 66n;
pay, 116; search for material for,
86, 138; *The Son of the Sheik*,
112, 117, 144; *Stella Dallas*
opening, 125; and talkies, 205;
and Valentino, 57, 71–72,
75–76, 96, 112; *The Winning
of Barbara Worth*, 116
Baragona, Margery, 207, 208,
211, 212, 213
Baragona, Tony, 194; chiropractic
medicine, 200–202, 204, 207;
death, 208; Los Angeles move,
178, 185, 189, 194, 195–97;
marriage to Valeria, 195–99,
203, 206–7; son, 207–8;
West New York, 165, 178,
185, 187–88, 189, 191
Baragona, Tony, Jr., 207–8, 211,
212, 213
Barnard, George Gray, 161
Barrymore, Ethel, 97
Barrymore, John, 55, 76–77, 198
Barrymore, Lionel, 123
Barthelmess, Richard, 140
Basquette, Lina, 180, 187, 190
Bauchens, Anne, 206

beach parties, 85

Beauty and the Beast, 108, 129, 144–45

Belletti, Valeria: asthma, 5, 159, 162, 186, 196, 198, 207; clothes, 17, 29, 34, 81, 85, 113, 114, 121, 124, 139, 141, 164; dancing lessons, 121, 131, 133, 141; death, 208; father, 3, 5, 128, 147–51, 156; golf, 15, 46, 98, 124, 177, 190, 206; height, 6; horseback riding, 14, 24–25, 33–34, 46, 53–54; Los Angeles arrival (1924), 3, 6–7; marriage to Tony Baragona, 193–99, 203, 206–7; mother, 3–5, 178, 203; New Jersey, 3–5; photo, ii; son, 207–8; writing interests, 70, 121, 138, 146–47, 149, 160–61. *See also* finances, Valeria's; jobs; lodgings; roommates; travel

Ben Hur, 55

Bennett, Belle, 49, 57–61, 71, 81, 83, 125

Berg, A. Scott, 20, 214

Berto, 153–54

The Best Years of Our Lives, 205

The Big Parade, 96

Black Pirate, 129

Blockade, 199

The Blood of the Conquerors (Fergusson), 183

Blue, Monte, 140

Boardman, Eleanor, 67, 125

"Bohemians," Los Angeles, 19, 100–108, 119, 129

Boland, Mary, 37

Bond, Carrie Jacobs, 135

Booth, Margaret, 206

bootleggers, 56, 212

Borden, Olive, 197

Bordighera, Italy, 150–51, 155, 157–59, 160, 162, 163

Borg, Carlo, 129

Bow, Clara, 63n, 146

Boyd, William, 140, 167, 179–80

Bradford, Virginia, 190

Brady, Alice, 36

Broadway: Bennett, 60; Colman, 23; Langner, 4; *Meet the Wife,* 37; *Tenth Avenue,* 175

Bromfield, Louis, 183

Bronson, Betty, 125

Broun, Heywood, 26, 30, 173

Bulldog Drummond, 205

Burkan, Nathan, 22

Byron, Lord, 94, 156

The Candle, 116

Carol, Sue, 180

Carr, Harry, 173

Castellano, Vittorio, 161–62

Catalina, 6, 37, 166, 178, 196

Cather, Willa, 91

The Cat's Meow, 89

Chandler family, 88

Chaplin, Charlie: and Marion Davies, 29, 84–85, 87, 117; *Gold Rush* premier, 28n, 55–56;

Goldwyn-Howard marriage dinner, 35; on Hearst's yacht, 36, 87; marriage to Lita Grey, 28, 36, 85, 89; Negri and, 118; *Stella Dallas* opening, 125; United Artists, 33n, 115

The Charlatan, 188

Chicago Opera Company, 183

Christmas, 105–11, 171–73, 200

Civilization, 86

Claire, Ina, 203–4

Clark, Howard, 113, 121, 134–35

Cody, Lew, 111

Coghlan, Junior, 190

Colman, Ronald, 16–17, 22–23, 30, 76; *Bulldog Drummond*, 205; *The Dark Angel*, 31, 40, 49, 57, 66; divorce, 27; fan mail, 112; Goldwyn-Howard marriage dinner, 35; *His Supreme Moment*, 27; *Kiki*, 105, 111; pay, 83, 105n, 116; photos, 32, 79, 100, 102, 143–44; search for material for, 86, 138; *Stella Dallas*, 49, 125; talkies, 205; *A Thief in Paradise*, 17, 27; *The Twins*, 35; and Valeria, 27, 43, 67, 94–95, 104–5, 111, 172; *The Winning of Barbara Worth*, 116, 143, 146

Companionate Marriages (Lindsey), 176–77

Compson, Betty, 99, 125

Coolidge, Calvin, 102

Cooper, Gary, 140,144, 145–46, 211

The Cop, 179–80, 181

The Copperhead, 123

Costello, Dolores, 140

Cowen, William, 197

Cowl, Jane, 46

Cukor, George, 40–41, 205

Culver City, 141–42, 143; DeMille Studios, 3, 122–24, 130, 181; MGM, 3; Washington Hotel, 140–43

Cytherea, Goddess of Love (Hergesheimer), 118n

Dana, Viola, 47

dancing lessons, 121, 131, 133, 141

Daniels, Bebe, 132, 140

The Dark Angel, 37, 91; Banky, 40, 49, 57, 66, 79; Colman, 31, 40, 49, 57, 66; Fitzmaurice, 71, 72, 91; midnight showing, 81, 85; preview, 71

Darling, Scott, 200

Davies, Marion, 101–2; Chaplin and, 29, 84–85, 87, 117; *The Dark Angel* preview, 71; *Gold Rush* premier, 55; Goldwyn-Howard marriage dinner, 35; Hearst and, 29, 36, 85, 86, 89, 101–2, 110, 139; Frances Marion scripts for, 23; Motion Picture Ball, 140; sisters, 87; and Valentino and Banky, 72; yacht party, 85, 87; *Zander the Great*, 35–36

Del Rio, Dolores, 140

DeMille, Cecil B., 3, 130, 166; directing *The Godless Girl*, 169, 176; Goldwyn and, 20–21, 122n; and talkies, 193

DeMille Studios, 3, 122–24, 130, 181; Christmas, 171, 172; *Hold 'em Yale*, 168, 169, 171, 174–75, 179; layoffs, 174, 179–80, 181, 184; Pathé buyout, 181; Valeria's job, 166–81. *See also The Godless Girl*

Desire under the Elms, 116

Desmond, William, 48

divorce law, New York, 28n, 41

Dix, Richard, 30

Donaldson, R. M., 174–76, 179

Dugan, Jimmy, 32, 44–46, 51–52, 97, 102

Duryea, George, 190

earthquake, Santa Barbara, 64

economics: Los Angeles, 2. *See also* finances, film

Edison, Thomas, 2, 192–93

Electrical Pageant, 48

Examiner, Hearst's, 88

Fairbanks, Douglas, 121, 198; *Black Pirate*, 129; Electrical Pageant, 48; *Gold Rush* premier, 55; Goldwyn-Howard marriage dinner, 35; Frances Marion scripts for, 23; *Stella Dallas*, 49, 66; United Artists, 33n, 50, 115

Famous Players–Lasky, 20–21

Fascists, Italy, 154, 155, 158

FBO, 2

Film Daily, 192–93

finances, film: Davies, 110; Edison company, 2; *Four Horsemen of the Apocalypse*, 75n; Goldwyn Productions, 21; Hearst, 102n, 110; *Hold 'em Yale*, 179; Ince, 86; Mayer, 102n; Sinclair Oil stock, 38, 51; *Stella Dallas*, 73; *The Winning of Barbara Worth*, 116. *See also* salaries

finances, Valeria's: apartments/ bungalows, 14, 15, 82; for clothes, 17, 29, 81, 121, 124, 164; house purchase, 183; Italy, 141, 149, 152, 156, 159–60, 163, 164, 175; for traveling, 98, 121, 124, 185. *See also* salaries

First National Studios, 21–22, 41, 144–45

Fitzmaurice, George, 16–17, 21, 77, 91, 145; and Arlen, 99; *Beauty and the Beast*, 108, 144–45; *Cytherea, Goddess of Love*, 118n; *The Dark Angel*, 71, 72, 91; and Florence Vidor, 28, 67; and Glyn, 64; *Gold Rush* premier, 55; *His Supreme Moment*, 27, 35; pay, 83, 145; search for material for, 86, 96; *The Son of the Sheik*, 112, 117, 144; and Valeria, 27–28, 67, 72, 91, 104, 115, 144; *The Winning of Barbara Worth*, 116

"flickers," 2

Florence (Valeria's friend), 18–19,

95, 98–99, 102–3, 110, 130;
Catalina, 37; and Charsky, 77,
78; East, 57, 63, 68, 77, 82,
142; eating schedule, 93; and
Hansen, 114, 121; horseback
riding, 24–25, 46; Italy, 161–
62; and John, 135; and Lentz,
68, 69; marriage, 133, 140,
194, 208; Mount Lowe, 24–25;
Thanksgiving, 100; Valeria's death,
208; Youngstown, Ohio, 144
The Flower of the Drama (Young), 70
Fountain, Leatrice Gilbert, 88
Four Horsemen of the Apocalypse,
75n
Fox, William, 19
Fox studios, 13, 19
F.P.A. (Franklin P. Adams), 26, 30,
173
Franklin, Miss, 15, 25–26, 79, 97
French language, 96, 158

Gable, Clark, 123n
Gang War, 197, 199
Garbo, Greta, 39, 99n, 193, 204n
The Garden of Allah, 50, 63
Garnett, Tay, 195
Gauntier, Gene, 205
gender issues. *See* women
Geraldine, 197, 199
Gibson, Hoot, 48
Gilbert, John, 41, 88, 125, 139,
203–4
Gilbert, Roland, 192
Gish, Lillian, 23, 39, 125
Gish girls, 118

The Glorious Apollo, 94
Glyn, Elinor, 55, 63–64; *The Dark
Angel* preview, 71; Hearst yacht
party, 87; *It*, 63n; *Three Weeks*,
63n
The Godless Girl: MacMahon novel
of, 189, 191, 195, 197; movie,
169, 171, 172, 176, 179–81,
193, 199
The Gold Rush, 28n, 55–56
Goldwyn, Frances Howard, 35,
40–42, 48, 55, 205; baby,
136, 161; death, 205; Hearst
party, 139; and Valeria, 42, 44,
49, 68, 79, 95, 98, 99, 104,
136–61
Goldwyn, Samuel, 19–24, 28,
39–40, 205; Academy Award
for Best Picture (1947), 205;
daughter Ruth, 21; death, 205;
Electrical Pageant, 48; marriages,
28, 35, 40–42; name changes,
20, 21; personal style, 23–24,
28, 42–43, 49, 72. *See also*
Goldwyn Productions
Goldwyn, Samuel, Jr., vii, 205
Goldwyn Productions, 21, 171,
172, 205; DeMille Studios,
122–24; Pickford-Fairbanks lot,
115, 117; process, 51–52;
United Artists, 62–63, 68, 80,
115; United Studios lot, 22,
27n, 57, 118n. *See also The
Dark Angel*; Fitzmaurice, George;
Goldwyn, Samuel; Goldwyn
secretarial job, Valeria's; King,

Goldwyn Productions (continued)
  Henry; Lehr, Abe; Marion, Frances; Stella Dallas
Goldwyn secretarial job, Valeria's, vii, 4, 16–18, 23–147, 211; car/chauffeur, 53, 93, 122–23; clothes, 17, 29, 34, 81; and Cooper, 144, 145–46, 211; and drinking, 52–53, 104–5; Frances Goldwyn and, 42, 44, 49, 68, 79, 95, 98, 99, 104, 136–37; Goldwyn's personal style, 23–24, 28, 42–43, 49, 72; Goldwyn meeting Valeria, 39; Goldwyn reference, 147; job description, 43–44; pay, 14, 17, 33, 45, 49–50, 68, 104, 116; plans to leave, 115, 121, 123, 129, 136–38, 141, 144
golf, 15, 46, 98, 124, 177, 190, 206
Gone with the Wind, 122n
Goodman, Daniel Carson, 87
Goodwin, Harold, 145
Gordon, Huntley, 112
Gottschalk, Louis, 71, 77
Grauman, Sid, 13–14, 47, 55
Grauman's Chinese Theater, 13n
Grauman's Egyptian Theater, 13–14, 47, 55, 96
The Green Hat (Arlen), 99n
Greenwich Village, 100–101, 106, 119
Grey, Lita, 28n, 36, 85, 89
Griffith, Corrine, 31, 77

Griffith, D.W., 33n, 86, 169n
Griffith, Raymond, 139–40
Grosset and Dunlap, 189n
Grot, Anton, 29–30, 34, 123–24, 129
grunion fishing, 62

Hale, Alan, 180
Hall, Mordant, 72–73
Halliburton, Richard, 188
Hanson, Lars, 39
Harding, Ann, 204
Hart, William S., 48, 86
Haver, Phyllis, 180, 190
Hearst, William Randolph, 33; The Dark Angel preview, 71; and Davies, 29, 36, 85, 86, 89, 101–2, 110, 139; Examiner, 88; finances, 102n, 110; Gold Rush premier, 55; Goldwyn and, 101–2; San Simeon ranch, 139; yacht party/Ince death, 85, 86–90
Heifetz, Jascha, 67n
Hergesheimer, Joseph, 117–18
Hersholt, Jean, 49
hiking, 85–86
Hill, George, 56
His Supreme Moment, 16, 27, 32, 34–35
Hold 'em Yale, 168, 169, 171, 174–75, 179
HOLLYWOODLAND sign, 3
Holt, Jack, 125
Hoover, Herbert, 102n
Hopper, Hedda, 90, 145, 211
Horn, Camilla, 198

horseback riding, 14, 24–25, 33–34, 46, 53–54
Howard, Frances. *See* Goldwyn, Frances Howard
How to Write and Sell Film Stories (Marion), 147f
Hoxie, Jack, 48
Hughes, Lloyd, 102
Hughes, Rupert, 125

Ida, 30, 38, 84, 94, 110
Ince, Thomas, 3, 22, 85, 86–90, 122n
Irma. *See* Prina, Irma
Isabel, 30, 84, 110, 114, 185–86
It, 63n, 146
Italian language: concert music, 37; Italian sculptor, 109; Los Angeles paper, 112; movie people using with Valeria, 67, 72, 91; Tolstoy's *Resurrection*, 157; Valeria using, 32, 50, 157, 158, 178
Italy: movies made in, 32, 50, 108; Valeria's family, 3; Valeria's father, 3, 5, 128, 147–51, 156; Valeria's finances, 141, 149, 152, 156, 159–60, 163, 164, 175; Valeria's first trip, 121–22, 124; 128, 138, 141, 144, 146, 148–64; Valeria's plans for second trip, 175

Jack, 165–66, 168, 170, 171, 180
Jazz Age, 5

The Jazz Age, 199
The Jazz Singer, 192
Jimmie, 165–66, 168, 170, 171, 180, 185
jobs, Valeria's: DeMille Studios, 166–81; Dr. Losell's assistant, 8–12; fired, 10–11; Langners' secretary, 4–6, 42, 180; Loeb, 11, 14, 16; after marriage, 207; Palisades Park office, 165; Pathé, 181–205, 206; salary, 14, 33, 45, 49–50, 68, 104, 116, 167, 169, 204, 213; script girl hopes, 112, 115, 206, 212. *See also* Goldwyn secretarial job, Valeria's
John, 119–20, 124–26, 128, 131–32, 135, 138–39
Jones, 98, 106, 113, 120, 131–32, 134, 139
Joy, Leatrice, 88, 116, 125, 167
Joyce, Alice, 49, 67–68
Julian, Rupert, 129–30, 140–41

Keaton, Buster, 33n, 55
Kempley, Chester C., 88–89
Kennedy, Tom, 190
Kent, James, 92, 101
Kerry, Norman, 139
The Keys to This City, 30
Kiki, 105, 111
King, Henry, 22–23, 51–52, 62–63; and Cooper, 145; Dugan as assistant director, 32, 45, 51–52, 97; *The Garden of Allah*, 50, 63; *Gold Rush* premier, 55; pay,

King, Henry (continued)
83, 116; *Romeo and Juliet*, 50;
secretary (Marie), 92; *Stella Dallas*, 7, 32, 58–61, 63, 71–75,
80–81, 125; and Valeria, 43,
45, 62–63, 67, 72, 112, 115;
The Winning of Barbara Worth,
116, 117
Kinkeads, Valeria boarding with,
170–73, 177, 182–98
Kirk, Helen, 166–68, 170–73,
175, 177
Kirkwood, James, 125

Ladd, Alan, 180n
Laemmle, Carl, 19
Langdon, Harry, 140
Langner, Herbert, 4
Langner, Lawrence, 4, 19, 62–63;
Loeb introduction, 11; *The Magic
Lantern*, 4; marriage, 82; play,
183; Praskin and, 187; Valeria's
job, 4–6, 42, 180
languages: French, 96, 158. *See
also* Italian language
La Plante, Laura, 139
La Rocque de la Rour, Rod: Banky
marrying, 66n; *Hold 'em Yale*,
168, 169, 171, 174–75, 179;
Negri and, 118
Lasky, Blanche, 20, 21
Lasky, Jesse, 19, 20, 21
The Leathernecks, 187, 199, 200
Lee, Lila, 125
Lehr, Abe, 20, 42, 95, 108; *His
Supreme Moment*, 35; preview
tickets from, 54; *Stella Dallas*, 51,
57–58, 59–60; and Valeria,
17, 30–31, 41, 104; *Zander
the Great*, 36
Leider, Emily, 211, 212
Lentz, Harry, 68–69
Lindsey, Judge, 176–77
Listen Baby, 199, 200, 201
The Little Princess, 23
Livingstone, Margaret, 87
Lloyd, Frank, 31
Lloyd, Harold, 48
lodgings, Valeria's, 82, 95–96;
apartments, 12–13, 14, 15, 82,
98, 120, 166, 197; boarding with Kinkeads, 170–73,
177, 182–98; bungalows, 14,
18–19, 62, 70; house purchase,
182–83, 184–85, 186; Santa
Barbara, 207; Washington Hotel,
Culver City, 140–43; Wilshire
district, 92–93; YWCA, 6–10,
82. *See also* roommates
Loeb, Joseph P./Loeb, Walker and
Loeb, 11, 14, 16, 17, 32–33
London: Fitzmaurice, 21; Goldwyn,
20; Valeria, 158
Long Beach, 196–98
Loos, Anita, 205, 212, 213
Loos, Mary Anita, 212
Los Angeles, 1–2; "Bohemians," 19,
100–108, 119, 129; population,
3. *See also* lodgings; moviemaking
Los Angeles Times, 87, 88, 173

Losell, Dr., 8–12
Love in the Desert, 199–200
Loy, Myrna, 205
Lubitsch, Ernst, 41, 125, 145
Lyons, Ben, 33, 114
Lytell, Bert, 140

MacAvoy, May, 140
Maccario, Giovanni, 155–56
MacKail, Dorothy, 76
Mackenzie, Compton, 183
Macpherson, Jeanie, 169, 171–72,
    185, 205
Madison, Cleo, 205
The Magic Lantern (Langner), 4
Man and Superman (Shaw), 135–36
Man Made Woman, 181
March, Fredric, 205
Margaret Herrick Library, Academy
    of Motion Picture Arts and Sci-
    ences, 211
Marion, Frances, 16, 23, 27, 134,
    147n, 205, 213; Beauchamp
    book about, 211; and Cooper,
    145–46, 211; Cytherea, God-
    dess of Love, 118n; Goldwyn-
    Howard marriage dinner, 35;
    Goldwyn's wife assisted by, 42;
    His Supreme Moment, 35; How
    to Write and Sell Film Stories,
    147n; husband, 35, 202–3;
    pay, 83, 116, 213; Potash and
    Perlmutter, 60; pregnant, 161;
    Stella Dallas, 32, 60–61, 73,
    74, 77, 80; and Valeria, 104,

146–47, 167, 169, 206; The
    Winning of Barbara Worth, 116;
    Zander the Great, 36
Marked Money, 190
Marmont, Percy, 76
Marshall, Armina, 82
Marshall, Charles, 183
Mayer, Louis B., 19, 21, 39, 102n.
    See also Metro Goldwyn Mayer
    (MGM)
Meet the Wife, 37
Meighan, Thomas, 26, 84
Menjou, Adolphe, 132
Metro Goldwyn Mayer (MGM), 3,
    19–20, 118–19; Gable screen
    test, 123n; Garbo, 39, 193; jobs
    for girls, 167, 168, 169, 176;
    layoffs, 174; The Scarlet Letter,
    39; talkies, 192, 193. See also
    Goldwyn, Samuel; Mayer, Louis B.
Millay, Edna St. Vincent, 36–37,
    38–39
The Missing Man, 199
Mission Inn, Riverside, 92
Moore, Colleen, 23, 77, 139
Moore, Owen, 67
Moran, Lois, 49, 66, 125
Moreno, Tony, 125
Morning World, 26
Morris, Kathleen, 108
Motion Picture Ball, Motion Picture The-
    atre Owner's Convention, 139–40
Motion Picture Patents Company. See
    the Trust
Mount Lowe, 24–25

moviemaking: Los Angeles beginnings, 2–3; process, 51–52; today, vii. *See also* studios; talkies

Murdock, J.J., 56

Murray, Mae, 125

Muschi, 106–7, 112, 119–20, 126–27, 131–32, 134–36, 206

My Antonia (Cather), 91

My Country, 167

Myers, Carmel, 140

Nagel, Conrad, 26–27

Naldi, Nita, 31, 54

Nancy (Valeria's friend), 18–19, 92, 98–99, 102–3, 110, 170; Catalina, 37; Christmas, 105–6, 173; eating schedule, 93; after Florence left, 57, 62, 63, 70; and Florida, 94; golf, 124; hiking, 85–86; horseback riding, 24–25, 46; marriage, 113, 120, 142, 194, 208; Mount Lowe, 24–25; and Muschi, 106, 107; renting from Valeria, 182, 184–85; shower for Valeria, 198; Thanksgiving, 100–101; Valeria's death, 208

Ned McCobb's Daughter, 197

Negri, Pola, 41, 112, 117–18

New Jersey. *See* West New York, New Jersey

Newman, Joe, 56

New Mexico, Valley Ranch, 79, 82, 133

New York: divorce law, 28n, 41; Greenwich Village, 100–101, 106, 119; *Stella Dallas,* 77, 81–82; Theater Guild, 4, 14, 70; Valeria's jobs, 4–6, 165, 180. *See also* Broadway; Langner, Lawrence; New York newspapers; West New York, New Jersey

New Yorker, 42

New York newspapers, 159; columnists, 26, 30, 173; *Morning World,* 26; *New York Daily News,* 87; *New York Times,* 72–73, 88, 89

Niblo, Fred, 55

Nice, France, 158

Nicholson, Bob, 78, 82–83, 100

Nineteenth Amendment, 5

Nixon, Marion, 140, 197

Noisy Neighbors, 199

novelizing, 189n

Office Scandal, 199

Olmstead, Gertrude, 140

O'Neil, Sally, 204

Orsellis, 132

Otis family, 88

Owen, Seena, 87

Paramount, 19, 22, 146

Paris: Fitzmaurice, 21; Moran, 49; Muschi's trip plans, 107; Valeria's trips, 98, 121, 124, 128, 148, 177

Paris Bound, 204

Paris Inn, 105–7, 113–14,119–
20, 124, 128, 134, 139
Parsons, Louella, 55, 89–90
Partners Again, 77, 91
Pascal, Ernest, 169
Pathé Studios: Christmas, 200; De-
Mille buyout by, 181; Fitzmaurice,
21; *The Godless Girl*, 176n,
181, 199; layoffs, 201; president
Murdock, 56; sold, 204–5;
talkies, 197, 199, 204; Valeria's
job, 181–205, 206
Pedretti (sculptor), 109, 112, 120
The Perennial Bachelor, 94
The Perils of Pauline, 21
Perinaldo, Italy, 148–63
Phantom of the Opera, 129–30
Philbin, Mary, 71, 139
Photoplay, 21
Pickford, Charlotte, 57
Pickford, Jack, 104, 197
Pickford, Mary, 21; *Gold Rush*
premier, 55; Goldwyn-Howard
marriage dinner, 35; Marion as
exclusive screenwriter for, 23;
marriages, 67; mother, 57; United
Artists, 33n, 50, 115
Pickford-Fairbanks lot, 115, 117
Pidgeon, Walter, 140
Poor Little Rich Girl, 23
Possession (Bromfield), 183
Potash and Perlmutter, 21, 60, 77
The Potboilers, 116
Praskin, Leonard, 187, 188
Prevost, Marie, 180
Prina, Irma, ii, 5–6, 208, 213

Pringle, Aileen, 118–19
prohibition, 56–57, 89
Prouty, Olivia Higgins, 61

Queen Kelly, 202
Quillan, Eddie, 197, 204

Raisa, Rosa, 183
The Rat, 96
Rebecca, 122n
Rebecca of Sunnybrook Farm, 23
Regan, James, 68
Replenishing Jessica (Rodenheim), 70
Richman, Arthur, 203
Riverside, Mission Inn, 92
RKO, 204
Roach, Hal, 129
road show pictures, 200
Robinson, Casey, 200, 201
Rochlen, A.M., 88
Rodenheim, Max, 70
Rome, 163–64
Romeo and Juliet, 46–47, 50
roommates, Valeria's, 14–15, 113,
139, 166, 168; Connie, 126,
130; Eva, 12–13, 14. *See also*
Florence; Nancy
Rostand, Giglio, 152, 154–56,
158, 162, 164
Rowland, Richard, 41
The Royal Road to Romance (Halli-
burton), 188
Rubens, Alma, 118n

St. Johns, Adela Rogers, 88, 147n
salaries, 83–84, 116; Banky, 116;

salaries *(continued)*
Bennett, 83; Colman, 83, 105n,
116; Cooper, 146; at DeMille,
167, 169, 175, 181–82;
Fitzmaurice, 83, 145; at Goldwyn, 14, 45, 49–50, 68, 104,
116; at Ince, 86; King, 83, 116;
Loos, 213; Marion, 83, 116,
213; Meighan, 84; at MGM,
167; at Pathé, 204; Schenk's secretary, 33; Swanson, 84; Valeria,
4, 14, 17, 33, 45, 49–50, 68,
104, 116, 167, 169, 204, 213
San Diego, 166; Ince death, 87,
88–89; Valeria and Irma trip, 6
Santa Barbara: earthquake, 64; Margery and Tony, 208, 211; Valeria
and Irma trip, 6, 64, 124; Valeria
and Tony move, 207
Saturday Evening Post, 118
The Scarlet Letter, 39
Schenck, Joseph, 21, 45, 91;
The Dark Angel preview, 71;
Goldwyn-Howard marriage
dinner, 35; married to Norma
Talmadge, 33n, 191–92; secre-
tary (Ruth Trolander), 32–33, 34,
93, 96, 115, 142, 180; and
Valentino, 75, 76n, 112; *Zander
the Great,* 36
Schildkraut, Joseph, 167
Schildkraut, Rudolph, 167
Schipa, Tito, 37
Selwyn, Edgar, 21, 41
Selwyn, Sonny, 79

Selwyn brothers, 21
Selznick, David O., 21, 122n, 204
Selznick, Irene, 21, 42
Sennett, Mack, 86
Sewall, Blanche, 206
Shady Lady, 199
Shaw, George Bernard, 37,
135–36
Shearer, Norma, 139
Sherwood, Robert, 205
Show Folks, 187, 190, 199
Shriners, 48–49
Sierra Hiking Club, 85–86
Sinclair, May, 46
Sinclair Oil stock, 38, 51
Singapore Sal, 190, 199
The Skyscraper, 180
Sonny, 22
The Son of the Sheik, 112, 117,
144, 148
Sony, 205
The Spieler, 195
The Spoiler, 199
Square Shoulders, 199
The Squaw Man, 20
Stella Dallas, 16, 36, 70–71;
Bennett, 49, 57–61, 71; cast,
49; Fairbanks, 49, 66; Joyce,
49, 67; King, 7, 32, 58–61,
63, 71, 73, 74–75, 80–81;
Marion, 32, 60–61, 73, 74,
77, 80; Moran, 16, 66; New
York theatres, 77, 81–82,
97–98; novel, 61; opening,
98, 101–2, 123, 125; pre-

views, 77, 80–81; process, 51–52; Valeria's disappointment with, 73–75, 77; Valeria's job and, 50

Steward, Anita, 125

Stiller, Mauritz, 39

Stone, Lewis, 27, 32, 54, 118n

Stroheim, Erich von, 125, 202

studios, 2–3, 19–22; DeMille, 3, 122–24, 130, 181; First National, 21–22, 41, 144–45; Fox, 13, 19; Ince, 3, 86; Paramount, 19, 22, 146; RKO, 204; Roach, 129; Sony, 205; Triangle, 21, 86; United, 2, 22, 118n, 122n, 145; Universal, 19; Warner Brothers, 2–3, 145, 174. *See also* Goldwyn Productions; Metro Goldwyn Mayer (MGM); Pathé Studios; talkies; United Artists

Sullivan, Gardner, 169

Swanson, Gloria, 55, 76n, 84, 202

Sweet, Blanche, 26

talkies, 192–93, 197, 199, 204, 205

Talmadge, Constance, 33, 42; *The Dark Angel* preview, 71; *Gold Rush* premier, 55; Goldwyn-Howard marriage dinner, 35; Frances Marion scripts for, 23; *The Twins*, 35; United Artists, 33n, 115

Talmadge, Natalie, 33n

Talmadge, Norma, 34, 42; *The Dark Angel* preview, 71; Electrical

Pageant, 48; *Gold Rush* premier, 55; Goldwyn-Howard marriage dinner, 35; *Kiki*, 105; Frances Marion scripts for, 23; married to Schenck, 33n, 191–92; United Artists, 33n, 50, 115

Talmadge, Peg, 42

Tarello, Mary, 77

Tearle, Conway, 26

Tellegen, Lou, 140

Tenth Avenue, 175

Terry, Bridget, 212

Thalberg, Irving, 19

Theater Guild, New York, 4, 14, 70

A Thief in Paradise, 17, 27

Thomson, Fred, 35, 202n

Three Weeks (Glyn), 63n

Thus Spake Zarathustra, 96

Tia Juana, 114–15, 166, 198

Tol'able David, 22

Toland, Gregg, 205

Tolstoy's *Resurrection*, 157

Tony. *See* Baragona, Tony

Tourneur, Maurice, 18

"Travel" (Millay), 38–39

travel, Valeria's: Hawaiian Islands plan, 177; honeymoon, 189, 190, 196; Italy, 121–22, 124, 128, 138, 141, 144, 146, 148–64; money saved for, 121, 185; Paris, 98, 121, 124, 128, 148; plans not carried out, 175, 177, 185, 207

Triangle Studios, 21, 86

Trolander, Ruth, 32–33, 34, 93, 96, 115, 142, 180
the Trust (Motion Picture Patents Company), 2
Turin, 158, 159, 161, 164
Turpin, Ben, 13
The Twins, 35

United Artists, 33n, 50; Goldwyn, 62–63, 68, 80, 115; Kiki, 105n; layoffs, 174; Pickford-Fairbanks lot, 115, 117; The Son of the Sheik, 117, 148; Sullivan, 169; Tony tour, 198
United Studios, 2; Goldwyn's company on lot of, 22, 27n, 57, 118n; mailing address, 57; secretaries for Cooper, 145; sold to Paramount, 122n
Universal City, 3
Universal studio, 19

Valentino, Rudolph, 47, 77, 91; and Banky, 57, 71–72, 75–76, 96, 112; The Dark Angel preview, 71; death, 148, 202n; Electrical Pageant, 48; funeral throngs, 202n; Leider biography, 211; Negri and, 112, 117–18; The Son of the Sheik, 112, 117, 144, 148; United Artists, 50, 115; wife Natasha, 47, 72, 75, 76n, 96
Valley Ranch, New Mexico, 79, 82, 133

Valli, Virginia, 54
Variety, 88
Velez, Lupe, 198
Vestal Fire (Mackenzie), 183
Vidor, Florence, 28, 41, 55, 67, 145
Vidor, King, 28, 67, 125
The Volga Boatman, 130
Von Stroheim, Erich, 125, 202

Warner, Sam, 180
Warner Brothers, 2–3, 145, 174
Washington Hotel, Culver City, 140–43
Weber, Lois, 205
West, Roland, 96
West New York, New Jersey, 50–51, 124; house, 3, 164–65; Tony, 165, 178, 185, 187–88, 189, 191; Valeria and mother, 3–5, 178
What Holds Men, 179–80
What Price Glory, 96
The White Sister, 22, 23
Winds of Chance, 31, 47
Windsor, Claire, 27, 140
The Winning of Barbara Worth (Wright), 116, 117, 129, 136, 144–46, 159
Winton, Jane, 35
Without Lying Down: Frances Marion and the Powerful Women of Early Hollywood (Beauchamp), 211, 212
A Woman of Affairs, 99n
The Woman who Lied, 54

women: emancipated, 183; glass ceiling/steel ceiling, 4, 115, 212; in movie business, 115, 205–6, 212; script girl hopes dashed, 115, 212; suffragette parades, 5

Women and Wives (Ferguson), 24

Woon, Basil, 56

Wright, Harold Bell, 116n

Wyler, William, 205

Yosemite, 189

Young, Stark, 70

Zander the Great, 35–36

Zukor, Adolph, 19, 20–21

TEXT	Futura Light & Bembo
DISPLAY	Futura Light & Edwardian Script
DESIGNER	Victoria Kuskowski
INDEXER	Barbara Roos
COMPOSITOR	BookMatters, Berkeley
PRINTER AND BINDER	Maple-Vail Manufacturing Group